GABRIEL A. FOSTER

The Fire Within

*grafo*house

TULSA | GUADALAJARA

The Fire Within
© 2025 by Gabriel A. Foster

Published by Grafo House Publishing
Guadalajara, Mexico | Tulsa, Oklahoma

ISBN   978-1-963127-27-0 (hardbound)
        978-1-963127-28-7 (paperback)
        978-1-963127-29-4 (ebook)

Cover design by Edgar Pulido

Printed in the United States of America
28 27 26 25   1 2 3 4

For Roseanne. Your steadfast belief in me has been life-changing. You've challenged me to never settle, be myself at all times, and never give up. It's your voice I hear in my head telling me to keep going. Thank you—for everything.

To Andrew, Evelyn, Daniel, Michael. I have long imagined that one day your little eyes will make their way onto the pages of this book. More than any other reader, I wrote this to you. I hope, by watching Dad step out onto a limb and try something new, you are inspired to live your own adventure. Dream big.

TABLE OF CONTENTS

THE INNER FIRE

You're living on the precipice of either the greatest victory or worst defeat in human history.

It's a scary and exciting thought: *this* moment is unlike any other. It's unique and the stakes are precipitously high. Modern society balances on a razor's edge, waiting for a push. A single person can plummet us into another civil war, anarchy, tribalism, and chaos. Conversely, one person, with God's power, can lead us into a beautiful and vibrant future.

What happens next is up to you—*no pressure.*

The course of history has often been changed by an individual. How can this happen? Like a spark igniting a forest fire, one person with inner fire can start a revolution. Far-fetched? Maybe. But a movement of consequence must be. To do anything of this sort, you must dream beyond the horizon of possible. However, there's an upfront cost: an average life. To be different and create monumental change, you'll need to walk an uncommon and narrow path. *Now* is your time.

In Paul's final letter to his protegé Timothy, he didn't hold back. He praised the faith of Timothy's mother and grandmother, but challenged him with these words:

> *Timothy, you have a gift only you can fan into flame.*[1]

This gift—like a flickering spark—needed to be stirred up, nurtured, and given attention. While his natural inclination was timidity, Paul urged him to walk with God's Spirit in boldness and power. Nobody else could do the work for him—not mom, grandma, or Paul. His spark—his God-given potential—was his own.

Like Timothy, your spark is your own, to fan or let die. God's put a gift in you. He's challenging you—right now—to step fully into how He made you. The world needs it and nobody else can do the work. Your life is bigger than you. While fanning your flame keeps you warm, helping others to do the same begets a *movement*. It's the nature of fire to spread.

God's Kingdom—what He is doing here on earth—is this movement. It's an incoming tide lifting the lives of everyone in its path. However, there exists an enemy—an opposing force—to you and any movement of this sort. This adversary seeks to extinguish your flame *one drop of water at a time* by keeping you in the confines of *possible*.

The strategy against you has been simple but effective: distraction, division, discouragement, and disengagement.

Drip…drip…drip.

The enemy will do whatever he can to convince you there's someone else to do the world-changing, to keep you on the sidelines without fighting to get in the game. Enough water and the spark is gone. It's a decent enough strategy because it keeps you playing defense. But there's a fatal flaw it doesn't account for: *you seeing it for what it is, waking up, and attacking it with a ferocity previously unknown.*

This book is for you if you're the type of person desperately searching for an inner fire and a calling bigger than yourself. If you want to meander through an easy and unchallenging life, you're kindly invited to put this down. But I don't think that's you. This is for the dreamers—those willing to put it all on the line, who want to make an impact on future generations. Now is your time.

Here are the four themes we'll explore:

One: oppressive forces are at play and working obsessively to drench and **steal your fire**. You've been sold an empty dream of the good life and live in a culture hell-bent on forming you into an isolated, angry, broken, and cynical individual.

Two: you need to **spark your fire**. You must experience an awakening—an opening to the Holy Spirit—which sets you on fire. This can *only* be found in and through Jesus' invitation to lose your life, follow him, and become his apprentice.

Three: to turn a spark into flame—and to keep your inner flame burning bright—you must train in the art of **strengthening your fire**. A physical fire grows with logs, oxygen, and fanning. Inner fire is no different. You need logs (a Rule of Life), oxygen (the Holy Spirit's empowerment), and fanning (effort to become like Jesus). The end goal isn't a spark that's here today and gone tomorrow. It's to foster an inner fire that burns bright eternally.

Four: sparking and strengthening your fire *isn't about you.*
The point is **sharing** what you have. God gives you his Spirit
to empower you to love him and others. This happens in
intentional small and large faith communities, where you'll
lead others to spark and strengthen their own flames. When
you allow God to transform your inner world, and train others
to do the same, you're entering a sacred way of life which is
exponentially larger than you.

Any movement of substance doesn't start from the top-down,
but bottom-up. It's always a collection of people—not laws,
programs, or systems—who produce change. We are these
people, who must become unified around a *righteous* cause. As
Philosopher Dallas Willard said:

> The revolution of Jesus…is a revolution of character.…[It]
> is one that changes…ideas, beliefs, feelings, and habits of
> choice…[2]

God—like an archer with a loaded arrow—aims intently at one
target through this book: *your inner transformation.* The goal is
complete inner life reorientation around the person of Jesus.
Nothing less will do. Again: if you don't want to be challenged,
this may not be for you. This will take everything you have.
Let's begin.

ONE
STEALING
YOUR FIRE

THE PRISONER IS ME

The silence was deafening in the cold wooden courtroom. With a loud crack, the side door swung open. In sauntered Josh, escorted by the bailiff. As he shuffled to his seat, his wrist and ankle shackles clanked and clattered. His eyes were distant, glued to the floor. Long and matted hair covered his head. He sent a chill up my spine every time I saw him.

Josh was here for felony assaults—*plural.*

A year earlier, in a Starbucks, he decided to randomly attack a woman waiting in line ahead of him. Then—in jail for the first assault—he beat up a much smaller inmate sitting in a holding cell. No one had any idea why he'd snapped either time, because he didn't speak the entire year he was in jail waiting for the cases to resolve. Not one word.

During the week-long trial, his attorney argued he should be unshackled to prevent bias (i.e., the jurors thinking he was guilty because he was shackled). Despite my objection—I argued the risk he'd snap *on me* outweighed any potential bias—the Judge agreed he should be unchained. As the State's lead prosecutor, I moved about the room carefully, always keeping an arm's reach away from Josh. His attorney's pen— conveniently left at all times on the desk—would make a formidable shank if I said something that angered him.

Suffice to say, I was glad trial was over. Josh was shuffling in to hear the verdict. As he sat, the Judge slowly unfolded the crisp piece of paper holding his fate. As he prepared to read it, time stood still. I glanced to my right at Josh's lawyer. He looked alive *and* lifeless all at the same time. Papers were strewn all over his desk and a loose-fitting tie sagged around his neck. His eyes were sunken and bloodshot, and stubble grew in patches on his face. I looked next at the 12 jurors, glued to their chairs like they were back in school before a big test. The tension was palpable.

"Guilty."

The verdict should have brought relief to my weary soul. In theory, justice had been served. This wasn't a difficult case— cameras captured both assaults clearly. The only issues were the extent of the injuries. I had to prove the damage to the victims was severe and long-lasting. If I did, Josh got a felony (as opposed to a misdemeanor). A felony meant more time in jail and probation, which seemed fair given the chilling attacks. "Ladies and gentlemen of the jury, thank you for your service," the Judge said in closing. He rose and swiftly departed.

I snuck one final glance at Josh, and our eyes met for the first time. It was only a few seconds, but I saw him in a new light. His eyes whispered a story I hadn't heard amid the noise of the trial. He wasn't a monster. No, he wasn't the ominous, wicked beast I painted him out to be to the jury. He was a hurting and scared little boy in a broken world. For the first time I saw him as *human*. I considered how knotted up he must be inside to do something so terrible to innocent people.

Unexpectedly, I connected with Josh. I, too, was a scared and hurting little boy in a big and broken world. I was no better, nor any worse. We stood on common ground. As the world pulled us our separate ways, this moment of unanticipated connection stuck with me. As deputies led him away, I left through a different door, our paths never to cross again.

I became a lawyer to *help*. The system is complicated and making it simple and accessible felt meaningful. If I'm honest, I also wanted a well-paying job and the respect which comes from telling people you're a lawyer at cocktail parties. However, even the most inspired attorney gets jaded working long enough. At the District Attorney's office, I moved up the ladder and took opportunities as they came. Life was moving fast, and I couldn't quite help but feel the shackles on my life getting tighter and tighter. *Where's your fire? Where's the passion that woke you up in the morning? Why are you limping through the day?* I cross-examined myself harder than I did to any defense witness.

After packing my files into a worn leather briefcase, I made the solitary trek down the cold marble courthouse stairs. The trial was over for the day, but tomorrow would bring a new tragedy to litigate. As I pulled into our driveway that evening, I realized how tired I was, in every sense of the word. My heart was still pounding a mile a minute from the adrenaline of trial, but my body was shot.

I slipped through the front door and my wife, Rosie, gave me the look. Her eyes said it all—another long day. Rosie was, and is, our rock. She holds our family of six together, but the pace and challenges of life were taking a toll on her, too.

After small talk, I slumped on the couch and tried to make myself invisible.

But our kids would have none of it. "Play?"

"Later baby." I turned on Netflix.

Eventually, everyone fell asleep. But my heart felt like a clenched fist, refusing to unfurl and relax. Years of pushing the limits were finally catching up to me. I put on a Liam Neeson movie in our living room to pass the time. As the night wore on, all of the "tomorrows" felt dark, like a black storm cloud traveling my way and gathering speed.

I wanted to be *done*.

Done with the rat race and chronic fatigue. *Done* with the mortgage, student loans, and credit cards. *Done* with the arguments, tantrums, and tragedies. I was in *way* over my head, and instead of sleeping, I was self-destructing while Liam Neeson beat up people on an airplane.

As the movie ended and the credits rolled, I stared blankly ahead. I felt a voice—maybe me, maybe God—whisper:

> *This isn't it. This isn't the life you want. What are you going to do?*

It took my breath away. *I don't know* was all I could muster as a meek response. What I did know was in a few hours, I'd wake up and do it all over again.

Life—a culmination of days, weeks, and years—can feel like a vicious and merciless cycle. We're stuck on repeat, living the same day, asking the same questions, praying the same prayers—but we don't have *the* answer. And as the saying goes, *nothing* changes if nothing changes. Nothing changed for me, except I started coping in unhealthier ways. I filled the days with more noise, activity, and indulgence to mask the pain and growing depression. Any crack in the day—any time to think or breathe—I'd impulsively grab for my iPhone.

As the months rolled on, my body started to break down. My left eye began twitching and my hands developed a tremor. In my windowless office one morning, I had an anxiety attack. More accurately, it had me. Nothing quite describes this season of life like that moment. A supervisor berated me over the phone for something I'd done wrong, and I froze. For the first time in my life, I couldn't push forward. I gently placed the phone down on the receiver, closed my laptop, and sat completely still as the tears began to flow.

The quiet voice returned: *You are lost, my friend. You have the world, but what about your soul?*

Our stories aren't supposed to be like this. Life isn't meant to be consumed with anxiety, fear, depression, and a desperate grasping for meaning. You've had moments—times you've heard God's quiet whisper—that have been different from mine. But while our stories are unique, our underlying desires are the same.

THE SHARED NEED
FOR MEANING

We all have a deep yearning to discover why we're here. How would you answer if I asked you why you're alive and gave you time to explain? What specific purpose does your life serve? How we answer this question is quite literally a matter of life and death. Viktor Frankl, a Jewish psychiatrist who in 1942 was sent to a Nazi death camp, observed:

> *The will to find meaning is the primary motivational force in man.*[3]

He saw those who didn't have a sense of meaning tragically perish in the death camps, their inner spark of life snuffed out by the venomous hatred of the Nazi guards. Without meaning, we lose the will to live.

Humans need meaning like we need air.

This is not a new idea—there's nothing new under the sun. While the specific era presents new problems—social media, modern-day slavery, political polarization, and so forth— fundamentally we're still asking the same questions:

> *What does it mean to be human? Why are we here? How can we live a good life?*

Internal and external challenges make it hard to find meaning. Internally, our souls are barraged and battered by discouragement. There's a cynicism sweeping the land as thick as dust on an old country road. Many feel they will *never* be free to pursue meaning because it's hard to see beyond the daily grind. Along with cynicism, we face a daily war against ourselves. There's an urge in us to operate out of greed, lust, pride, anger, and idolatry (i.e., putting things in the position of God). Given this internal bent, we must fight to discover meaning.

In addition, there are larger external forces at play which also pull us away from the pursuit of meaning. There are concerning problems with the systems, governments, businesses, organizations, and communities we live in. All of these larger problems are simply the result of our internal realities. Our inner bent makes its way into everything we create, producing external systems rife with injustice, poverty, exploitation, hatred, and dehumanization. To put it simply: we're messed up on the inside, so we make messed-up systems. What are we to do?

To see a revolution of heavenly proportions, start by looking in the mirror. Without a reimagining of our inner life, we're chopping at branches which will only grow back. In other words, if we only focus on changing systems "out there," we never get to the root of the issue "in here"—our hearts. Certainly, external systems and corrupt laws need reformation. However, for *lasting* change, one must renovate the source, not the symptoms. Like one molecule causing a chain reaction in chemistry, God can use one person's transformed life—set on fire for his purposes—to fan the flames of a much larger movement.

Tolstoy wrote:

Everyone thinks of changing the world, but no one thinks of changing himself.[4]

To change yourself is to change the world. And part of this internal change is recognizing the idols you're pursuing. Our first stop: an examination of Western culture and how it seeks to drench our inner fire and pursuit of meaning by placing idols in front of us—yet always out of reach—like carrots on a stick.[5]

AMERICAN IDOL

In the West many idolize the American Dream and see it as our meaning for living. We look at life through an individualized lens in which we conflate the Dream with our purpose for being alive. For many, life is exhaustion, living paycheck to paycheck, working for the weekend, and striving for the good life—the carrot—that's always *just* out of reach.

Others are less fortunate and live below the poverty line, constantly working multiple jobs to make ends meet. Many more have lost their health and simply dream of walking again.

On the other end, some have more than enough financially, but live in crippling depression. Thoreau said:

The mass of men [and women] lead lives of quiet desperation.[6]

This applies across a wide range of circumstance and fortune. While our stations in life vary, we all feel an underlying anxiety because we don't know why we're here.

Corporations and influencers prey on our desperate search for meaning by peddling get-rich-quick schemes and a lavish lifestyle as "the answer." But meaning is something money can't buy. Those who are wealthier than ever still face isolation, depression, and suicide. How can this be?

Many, especially those in their 20s, 30s, and 40s, begin awakening to life's bigger questions: *Is how I'm living meaningful? Am I really finding fulfillment in what I'm doing?* Meanwhile, many disenfranchised groups battle to simply exist and are unable to entertain life's bigger questions. Survival requires focus on getting the next meal. And in this sense, we should honor and recognize that even having this conversation about meaning is a privilege.

Let's begin with how we've attempted to answer the question of meaning in America over the last century.

CROSS-EXAMINING OUR COLLECTIVE "WHY"

Why do we exist? Our response to this question determines everything we do and how we live, at least according to popular thought.[7] The American Dream was the *why* for many decades. It's essentially a to-do list with guarantees: *If you work hard and check all the boxes, you'll live happily ever after.* The basic checklist is: get good grades, graduate college, land a good job, buy a home, get married, have kids, work for 40 years, and retire at 65. If you do these things, according to the Dream, you'll have a good life.

None of these goals are inherently *bad*, but when they become the purpose for living—an answer to our collective why—they fall incredibly short. Money, degrees, titles, and possessions cannot buy happiness. Actor Jim Carrey once said:

> *I think everybody should get rich and famous and do everything they ever dreamed of, so they can see it's not the answer.*[8]

Most people can't check the boxes even if they tried. When we idolize the Dream, we see life as an individual endeavor, with the end goal of personal success. There's no value in community if the point is checking *my* boxes as quickly as possible. In this climb to success, people are either hindrances or stepping stones to be used for personal gain. It can be disheartening for a person who idolized the Dream to check all the boxes and retire at 65—lonely and none the happier—knowing they statistically only have 19 years left to live (the average age of death for those who reach 65 being 84).⁹ Happy thoughts coming soon…

I was privileged enough to check many boxes at a relatively young age. I grew up with several advantages: gender, skin color, my dad being a lawyer, both parents staying married, and being an only child, to name a few.¹⁰ I finished high school, college, and law school, and I married, worked as an attorney, owned a home, and started a family by my mid-20s. Again, to be clear, these are good things which become bad when we idolize them as *the* way to live a meaningful life.

Unfortunately, that's exactly what I did.

JESUS' ALTERNATIVE PLAN

Perhaps what you've idolized has been different—it likely is if you grew up in a different culture or socio-economic status than mine. However, our underlying need is the same: to live well. Whether you grew up in China, Chile, Chirala, or Chicago, this is what you're ultimately trying to do.

Jesus—in a worldwide competition with all known frameworks for life—simply offers the best response to this need. In a desert of despair, he is an oasis of hope. He doesn't provide a new program, diet, multi-level marketing scheme, or business to take from you—he offers to give you a new way to be human. Idolizing the Dream implores us to frenetically climb the ladder of success. Jesus invites us the opposite direction—to follow him on a downward trek into a life of simplicity, beauty, and depth.

He invites us into a life of meaning.

We inherently understand the things that make life meaningful. In his article "The Moral Bucket List," New York Times columnist David Brooks examines how we celebrate "eulogy virtues."[11] In other words, when a person passes, we universally consider whether they were:

...kind, brave, honest, or faithful. Were [they] capable of deep love?[12]

We don't celebrate their possessions, titles, or resumés. We look at their legacy in terms of impact on others. Death gives clarity to a meaningful life in this sense.

Brooks also wrote *The Second Mountain,* a book premised on the idea that life consists of two mountains.[13] The first mountain most attempt to climb—and perhaps do—is individual success. In the beginning of life, we're generally focused on upward mobility, careers, and success. However, one of two things happen. We either climb the mountain and find it empty at the top or get knocked off the path along the way. In either event, Brooks contends this moment (of summit or failure) reveals a "second mountain"—an entirely different life of faith, community, and calling—which comes into view as we leave the first. That mountain—which I argue is Jesus' life available to you and me—is the meaningful life you've been so deeply yearning for.

Let's keep exploring this idea. If a meaningful life consists of other-centered virtues we celebrate at funerals, along with faith, community, and living out one's calling, the next question is naturally how to start in that direction. Many make a living peddling life-hacks, training programs, meditation tips, and self-help books as attempts at an answer.

But again—while none of these are bad—they aren't *the* answer.

We can't life-hack our way into a meaningful life any more than we can *try* our way up Mt. Everest. Wouldn't it be great if—during my kids' seventeenth fight of the day—I could go into a closet, close my eyes, and transform myself into a more patient person by saying, with emphasis, "Be more patient"? That's not how it works.

To live a life meaningful to God, ourselves, and others, we must adopt a lifestyle.

We inherently understand the concept that to be like someone, we must embrace their way of living. To become a great athlete, one must train like the greats. To become a human of meaning, one must practice The Way of Jesus—who lived the most peaceful, joyful, and loving life in human history.

His open invitation is for exactly this: a way of life. It's a call to be a student shaped and formed into a new person. He isn't interested in getting you to *only* give intellectual assent to a set of doctrinal beliefs. This lifestyle can't be attempted through sheer willpower—it's too hard. Think about Jesus' description of the life of a follower in the Sermon on the Mount. Many consider it an impossible moral standard. But it is possible. To follow him—to do what he says—requires yielding to power beyond our own: the Holy Spirit.

Before you get dismissive and say I'm drinking the Kool-Aid, hear me out. We may think we're free-thinkers, marching to the beat of our own drums, but nobody *really* is. There is no such thing as a religious "none" (a person who doesn't follow anyone and holds no beliefs). You might not know it, but you are following *someone* and being formed into their image by adopting their practices (i.e., lifestyle).

Everyone is a disciple of someone. The question is not whether you are being discipled—it's by whom. And a second question closely follows the first: what kind of person are you becoming as a result?

Let me say it again: everyone is a disciple of someone. Dallas Willard wrote:

Terrorists as well as saints are the outcome of spiritual formation. Their spirits or hearts have been formed. Period.[14]

Simply put, you are a disciple, whether you know it or not. Discipleship and inner formation are inescapable realities of the human condition.

So, if you're going to follow someone, why Jesus and not Buddha, Alexander the Great, or Elon Musk? In part, if we choose anyone not named Jesus, they have a shadow side. As

Morgan Housel puts it in his book, *Same as Ever*, if you follow someone for the things you like about them and want to get those things, you're signing up for the whole package—not just the parts you like.[15] If you idolize Elon Musk and want his wealth and power, you necessarily also need to adopt his stress levels, workload, lack of privacy, and so on. You can't take the good without the bad.

The same features which allow great leaders to excel professionally can be damaging personally. There's a hidden cost to discipleship of anyone not named Jesus. We could go down the line, but you'll always find the same thing: following an imperfect human being will form you into someone you don't entirely want to become. *Everyone* has a shadow side and imperfections.

Jesus is the only person to ever live who didn't have this. His is the only lifestyle worthy of complete emulation. While there is a cost to following him, the life we find can only be described as *life and life to the full*.[16] Jesus led the most beautiful, profound, and resounding life in the history of the world—no one holds a candle to his light.

How did he live like this? Your first instinct may be to think it's because he was God. Subsequently, you may feel this kind of life is out of reach for you, because you are not God. However, and this is key, this kind of meaningful life is not only possible with the Holy Spirit—it's the natural outcome.

When you follow Jesus, you become a person who would do the kind of things he did, think the way he thought, and love the way he loved.

We must wrap our minds around the idea that it is entirely possible to become like Jesus.

He did have to exert effort to this end. While he was God, he also needed to constantly pray, fast, and engage in spiritual practices. Why do these things if he didn't need to? One argument may be that he simply intended to model them for us. But it seems his efforts to follow God were more than a model. I'm convinced God (the Son) came to earth fully human (while also remaining fully God). By doing so, he made himself dependent on God (the Father) to show us how to live with God (the Spirit). Accordingly, he built his lifestyle completely around connection with God and, as a result, lived with constant inner *peace* and *joy*.

He promises us *the same*, but it's going to take a fundamental reorientation of how we approach life.[17] If we aren't experiencing peace and joy while we follow Jesus, as my friend Walter says, *either Jesus was lying, or we're missing something.*

DECONSTRUCTING: FIVE WAYS OUR IDOLS DEFORM US

Let's deconstruct the idol of the American Dream. Again: not evil—just not *foundational*. By the same logic, bubble wrap isn't evil, but if you try to use it as foundation for a house, you're in for a long day. It's the same with our lives. It's good to have goals and aspirations. However, when they become our reason for living (i.e., idols), we've put them in a place to do what they cannot (provide meaning).

While there are many different ideas of what the Dream is, according to Oxford's Dictionary the definition is:

> *Everyone should have an equal chance to succeed and enjoy prosperity through initiative, hard effort, and drive.*[18]

To paraphrase, *everyone who works hard should be equally able to do well.*

James Adams first coined the term in 1931, during the Great Depression, and it began as a noble idea.[19] However, over time it has become perverted into an idol.

As decades passed, technology, consumer goods, and advertisements morphed the Dream into a checklist for meaning. It's no coincidence we're now subject to 10,000 advertisements a day from advertisers spending trillions trying to shape our minds around an idea of the good life (so we buy their product).[20] To say it another way, the Dream has become intertwined with a "successful lifestyle," which marketing companies define. Meaning (i.e., success) is now equivalent for many with owning certain things like a single-family home in the suburbs, a nice car, and fashionable clothes.

It would take a whole book to unpack this, and I'm wary of painting with such broad strokes in an attempt to summarize the complexities of humanity. However, what we do know is if we idolize the Dream, which now defines success as having certain things, it does something to us internally.

Let's look at five ways idolizing the Dream can deform our day-to-day lives: finances, hurry, relationships, mental health, and cynicism.

Finances

Companies play with your desire to be seen, known, and loved by selling a joyful lifestyle (which conveniently includes their product). It's a bait and switch. Their end goal isn't you living a life of joy—it's creating a repeat customer. If their product truly satisfied, we wouldn't need to buy more. That's not what they want.

As they play on our desires, we buy endlessly, digging ourselves into a deeper and deeper financial pit. Dave Ramsey said it like this:

> We buy things we don't need with money we don't have to impress people we don't like.[21]

The ensuing financial pressure we live with crushes our internal well-being.

In the 1950s, a high school graduate could earn a living wage, buy a house and car, and support a family of five on a single income. Of course, there were problems then, but the point is that lifestyle is now beyond reach for everyone outside the top one percent. The middle-class lifestyle previously available to many is all but gone.

Here's one reason why: things are *so* expensive now. Groceries, let alone education, cost exponentially more due to the rise in inflation. The cost of attending college is up *1,200 percent* since 1980.[22] If you have an undergraduate degree, you owe $39,000 on average when you graduate.[23] If you have a Master's, $84,000. A Ph.D.? $125,000.[24] These are *valuable* degrees, and college is an invaluable experience if you're able to attend. However, if you feel pressured to attend college to check a box based on idolizing the Dream, student loan debt presents a real challenge.

Another battle is the cost of homeownership. The average mortgage used to be twice as much as a person's annual income—now it's 3.5 times more.[25] The alternative and increasingly popular route is living at home for an extended period of time (if this is an option). In 1960, 10 out of 100 people between ages 18 and 34 lived with their parents. Now? *52 out of 100.*[26] The rise in living at home isn't *bad* as much as it's an observation that homeownership is increasingly challenging. In 1981, the median age of first-time homebuyers was 28.5. Now, it's 33.[27]

According to Ramsey Solutions, 77 percent of American households have at least some debts.[28] When life happens, in the form of home repairs, sickness, babies, injuries, and everything in-between, and we're highly leveraged financially, it goes on the card.[29]

Overall, financial pressure doesn't exist in a vacuum. When we idolize a certain lifestyle and let that determine our financial decisions, it can take a toll, leading to stress, divorce, escapism, and, tragically, suicide.

Hurry

Time is the great equalizer. We each get 1,440 minutes per day, no more and no less. However, while the amount of time we get hasn't changed, how we use it has. The pace at which we live is faster than ever. It hasn't always been like this. In the 1960s leading sociologists predicted that the emergence of time-saving technology would produce a more leisurely lifestyle in the future. In 1967, a U.S. Senate subcommittee jointly predicted that by 1985, the average American would work *22* hours a week, *27* weeks a year.[30] Things haven't panned out exactly like they thought. The opposite happened—we have more time-saving technology than ever *and* are also busier than ever. What gives?

They didn't account for human nature.

If we live under the premise that climbing the ladder leads to a good life, we'll climb as fast as we can. The more time technology saves us, the more time we devote to work. We don't take time for leisure because there is always *more* to earn and achieve. There is never "enough" when we idolize the Dream. And climbing the ladder fast requires sacrifices. Our health, boundaries, and relationships suffer as the result of continually living at an unsustainable pace.

John Mark Comer, author of *The Ruthless Elimination of Hurry* (and many other amazing books), identified three historical events which contributed to the present era of hurry.[31]

First, the public clock tower arrived in 1370. Before it, people rose and slept with the sun. A public clock system led to a man-made machine telling us when to rise and sleep, not the natural rhythm of seasons, sun, and moon.

Second, 500 years later—in 1879—Thomas Edison invented the light bulb.[32] Before the light bulb, the average person slept *10 to 11 hours per night*. Exactly 100 years after the light bulb (1979), the average amount of sleep had decreased by 20 percent (to approximately eight hours a night). Now? We sleep less than seven hours a night (and 33 percent sleep less than six).[33] Chronically tired and addicted to caffeine? Maybe it's because we're living at a faster pace on 40 percent less sleep than our great-grandparents.

Third, in 2007, Apple sold its first iPhone *and* social media platforms Facebook and Twitter took off. Over the past two decades, smartphones have become permanently attached to our hands, and we have *treatment centers* for social media addiction. Things escalated quickly.

The best minds in Silicon Valley *purposefully* make this technology incredibly addictive. Tristan Harris, a former Google product manager, explained how programmers design phones, apps, and social media to "hack your brains" and get you hooked.[34] Sound Orwellian? What's crazy is *we know this* and still use the products. They're *that* addictive. Next time you open a social media app, start counting the ways it's built to create compulsive behavior (likes, shares, Reels, the content they show, etc.).

This technology addiction leads us to fill every gap of spare time on our phones. The average iPhone user touches, swipes, and taps their phone *2,617* times per day.[35] Millennials spend on average four hours a day on their phones—amounting to *60 days a year* (15 percent of the year).[36] Gen Z, on average, spends *nine hours a day* in front of a screen. While this can be attributed in part to work and school, it's still a startling number. Every gap in the day we used to have to think, walk, process, and breathe is now full.

There's more, but this is the culture we live in which contributes to a chronic sense of hurry. Doctors have a name now for this *disease*: hurry sickness.[37] It's the state of being perpetually hurried, which destroys our ability to connect with God and others.

Relationships

C.S. Lewis observed:

> *Friendship is unnecessary, like philosophy, like art, like the universe itself....It has no survival value; rather it is one of those things which give value to survival.*[38]

If Lewis is right, what would the state of our friendships today say about us? Our capacity to relate with others has been *shattered* for several reasons (some of which we've already covered). Financial pressure can lead to working longer hours, stress, and jealousy (of those who don't have to overwork). Hurry means less time to relate. Throw in online learning, the meteoric rise of social media, and political polarization, and you get a group of 20- to 40-year-olds starving for friendship.

How, you may be thinking, can people be wanting connection? Aren't we connecting online more than ever? Isn't that illogical? Vehemently: *No.* Connections online in places like social media (via likes, comments, etc.) generally don't involve any relational depth. We think we're connecting, but it's at such a shallow level that when we leave the online world, we find we feel even more alone and unseen. We're interacting with a mask or filter, presenting an image of our real selves. Comments and likes cannot replace the depth of in-person connection—or even come close.

It's not a slam on us as much as it's a critique of this individualistic culture. In 2023, U.S. Surgeon General Dr. Vivek Murthy issued an 81-page report on the most dire epidemic facing Americans. Terrorism? Another pandemic? No. *Loneliness.*[39] Dr. Murthy revealed *60 percent* of Americans are lonely. In any room you enter, two-thirds of the people are in a friendship desert. Let that sink in. The effects of loneliness on our health are equivalent to smoking 15 cigarettes a day. Why? Socially connected people live longer.

All the way back to the creation story, God has told humankind: *It isn't good for you to be alone.*[40]

While connection is good for our health, we're disconnected because we've normalized transactional relationships. Philosopher Martin Buber, in his bestselling book, *I and Thou,* described how this works. Essentially, in a culture all about individual advancement, we tend to treat people as items (as an "it"—an object) rather than human beings ("thou").

When our understanding of a meaningful life is personal success only, we can easily justify using people as means to reach our ends. We no longer treat others as humans made in the image of God (whether it be girlfriends, baristas, store clerks, gas station attendants, parents, or peers). They're objects to use for our gain (be it sex, coffee, groceries, gas, money, a good laugh—the list goes on). In this commodified culture, we dehumanize each other constantly, leaving us lonely. Loneliness, as many know, is a dangerous place to be.

Mental Health

If we idolize the Dream, we embrace the grind. But we lose our minds in the process. While working hard is good, chronic overwork kills us. The stress we take on in an attempt to attain meaning can include financial pressure, hurry, and isolation. This cocktail does a number on our mental well-being.

Higher education is a good example of this dynamic. David Brooks writes about UCLA researchers who surveyed incoming college students about what they wanted from life.[41] In 1966, nearly 90 percent of students said they attended college to develop a meaningful philosophy of life. In 2000, only 42 percent maintained that motivation. Instead, the most important goal became being well-off financially. In 2015, 82 percent of students said financial success was primarily what school was for. And in 2018, Pew Research asked Americans what gives them meaning in life, to which only seven percent said helping other people, and 11 percent said learning.[42]

The mindset we take into any endeavor (like school) greatly determines how we go about the process. If the purpose of school is only to help us earn more later, we'll sacrifice our personal health to no end to achieve that goal.

Professor Adam Grant, in his book *Hidden Potential*, claims students in particular forfeit their mental health for the sake of "success."[43] In America, students at high-achieving high schools are clinically depressed and anxious at rates *three to seven times higher* than the national norm.[44] In China, students are pressured to be perfect and study long hours. Consequently, they top the academic charts for performance but are among the bottom 10 countries in life satisfaction. Over half of Chinese students reported feeling sometimes or always miserable. Over 75 percent felt sometimes or always sad.[45] On college campuses, anxiety and depression have skyrocketed. Nearly half of college students report symptoms of depression and anxiety.[46]

What are the root causes of such strain on our mental health? In part, we're buying into an idea that we must embrace a lifestyle of habitual sacrifice (in unhealthy ways) to enjoy life later. Again, working hard isn't bad. But there's a point at which "the grind" becomes unhealthy and damaging.

What's devastating is the youth who "succeed" by climbing the ladder never learn how to set boundaries and say no to work. Their mindset is to just "get it done" and land a good job. What they don't realize is they've jumped out of the academic frying pan and into the fire. For instance, the mental health of lawyers and doctors—some of the most esteemed jobs—is dismal.

A Mayo Clinic study found over half of physicians in a physician health program abused alcohol and over a third abused opioids.[47] A different study showed they abused prescription medications as a method to relieve stress and emotional or physical pain.[48]

In the legal field, it's no different. One in five lawyers are regarded as "problem drinkers," according to an American Bar Association poll of over 13,000 attorneys.[49] That's double the rate of other professionals with a similar level of education. The same study showed younger lawyers (practicing for 10 years or less) had the highest rates of substance abuse and mental health problems. From personal experience, what I saw looked a lot like burnout across the legal field.

If we approach life as if it should always be a graph moving upwards and to the right, we'll quickly sacrifice our mental health on the altar of success to get there.

Cynicism

There's a sweeping distrust of organized religion which harms more than it helps. We now live in a post-Christian culture that sees the church establishment as outdated and patriarchal. Many believe they can be the spiritual captain of their own ship without the dogma and hypocrisy of a local faith community. In this sense they idolize individualism over a faith community. However, this cynicism leads many to throw out the baby (Jesus and healthy faith communities) with the bathwater (abusive forms of organized religion).

Forty years ago, it was the norm to attend church. That has steadily eroded, with attendance in decline for decades. In 1999, 70 percent of U.S. adults said they belonged to a church, according to a Gallup survey. By 2020, the number decreased to 47 percent.

Why the decline? There's not one answer, but while researching I was struck by a conversation on Reddit, an anonymous online discussion forum. It was titled "Why does Gen Z experience declining religiosity?"[50] In so many words, users shared stories about hypocrisy, cruelty, and abuse they'd witnessed in church.

The behavior of Christians was the primary stumbling block to Gen Z—not Jesus.

Many in their 20s, 30s, and 40s feel stuck between a rock and a hard place: disassociate from church because of what they're seeing (and face spiritual isolation) or return to church (and face hypocritical Christians, Christian nationalism, etc.). Of course this doesn't capture everyone's experience and viewpoint, but it is a fear of many in the younger generation.

These are a few factors shaping the cultural waters in which we swim. Idolizing the American Dream is a game we lose *if* we choose to play. In the midst of it all, we're struggling to find a flicker of hope. You may be nodding along, agreeing with the problems that many aspects of our culture present. But it's not enough to agree with the problems. We need an alternative framework to live by. Let's turn to the next topic.

TWO
SPARKING YOUR FIRE

JESUS' GOOD NEWS

It's not about you.

Society would have you believe you're the center of the universe, but Jesus flips this on its head. His invitation is to an upside-down way of life—a Kingdom—where less is more, weakness is strength, and loss is gain. He taught an equation to life most find challenging to understand: things lead to their opposites. Humility leads to exaltation, surrender births freedom, restraint is pleasure, and death begets life.

It's with this understanding he invited everyone to follow by uttering these simple words:

> Whoever wants to be my disciple must deny themselves, take up their cross, and follow me. For whoever wants to save their life will lose it, but whoever loses their life for me will find it.[51]

To those who do this, he promises an inner awakening by God's Spirit:

> You will have water that will become a wellspring within you that gives life throughout eternity. You will never be thirsty again.[52]

This rebirth is "the spark." Sparking your fire isn't about God helping you achieve *your* goals—it's about aligning to God's Kingdom values to pursue his.

Here's where Jesus' invitation gets interesting. The gospel preached in the West is usually a variation of:

*God loves **you**.*
*But **you're** a sinner.*
*So Jesus died for **you** to erase **your** sin.*
***You** can choose to accept his gift—salvation.*
*Once **you** do, **you're** forgiven and set free.*

Additionally, many contemporary worship songs center around what God does for *us*, as if he only exists to serve us, not us him. John Mark Comer describes this gospel in *Practicing the Way* as true but incomplete.[53]

The focus is only on *you* and *Jesus dying*. In this you-centric version of faith, *we entirely miss Jesus' invitation to follow and become like him*. It in no way decreases the significance of Jesus' death and forgiveness of our sins to say there's more to following him than being forgiven. Those who hear this "forgiveness-only gospel" feel no need to go further and actually do what Jesus taught. If all we hear is that Jesus died to pay for our sins, there's no reason to try and do what he said.

This Westernized gospel is part—but not all—of what Jesus taught. For three years, he preached with a consistent theme:

Repent, for the kingdom of heaven is at hand.[54]

This was Jesus' sermon. *This* is his invitation to you and me.

As Dallas Willard writes in his book, *The Scandal of the Kingdom* (worth quoting at length):

> *Jesus preached that the Kingdom of God is now available. It was not about to happen, it was happening. When he preached that it was "at hand," he meant it in the way you might lead someone using your hands into your dining room. He's saying that with him as your guide, you can easily turn and walk into the Kingdom. He brought the Kingdom of God in his person into the lives of those around him so they could experience it through his presence in their lives. Jesus put a face to the Kingdom of God.*[55]

Jesus is the Kingdom embodied, the perfect representative of this new way of life. Through him, God revealed to us a new way to be human—available right at our fingertips. When we accept his invitation to follow—to live a Kingdom life—we become fire-carriers (vessels) who reveal the Kingdom of God to everyone we encounter. If you're feeling somewhat lost, let's return to the big idea:

To only focus on Jesus' death is to miss his invitation to follow (i.e., to live a Kingdom-oriented lifestyle with God).

Reducing him to someone who *only* came to die fails to see how he showed us to live.

It's common in the West, under this forgiveness-only gospel, to view eternal life as available *later*—when we die. With this perspective, a Christian's life becomes focused on escaping the world and running out the clock so they can be with Jesus in eternity. Heaven is anywhere but on earth, right?

Well, Jesus himself offers eternal life now (a life of the utmost quality) and later (a life in unending quantity). In the only portion of Scripture where Jesus explained eternal life, he described it as *knowing God and himself*.[56] If this is eternal life, we can experience it here and now *and* forevermore.

Through following Jesus' lifestyle (which showed the Kingdom to those he encountered), we too begin to reveal the Kingdom of God to others. With a Kingdom mindset, our lives become vessels through which God works to make earth as it is in heaven.

Jesus constantly preached, taught, and performed miracles, signs, and wonders to reveal this inbreaking Kingdom. To *only* focus on his death is to miss the forest for the trees (i.e., to miss what he said, demonstrated, and modeled about Kingdom life).

Am I saying not to appreciate his death and resurrection, critical aspects to his invitation? Not at all—but he wasn't the only person to die and be raised from the dead. In the scriptural narrative, many died and were resurrected (Lazarus and Dorcas, for example).

The reason we worship Jesus—and not Lazarus or Dorcas—is because of what *he claimed his death and resurrection meant.* He said he was the Son of God here to usher in a new reality—a Kingdom—through his life, death, and resurrection. He said that by going away, an Advocate (God's Spirit) would come to live in all his followers.[57] These are unique claims.

To Jesus, God's Kingdom wasn't an abstract idea; it was something you could *experience* internally and everywhere you went. Again, the Kingdom is what God is doing and life as God intends: with his Spirit, full, peaceful, just, abundant, and loving. It's bringing to earth—and to you—what's already happening in Heaven.

We encounter this Kingdom through a relationship with Jesus, when we put trust in who he said he was and what he came to do. In this sense, we enter on an individual level. But Jesus' vision involves more than isolated people putting trust in him.

The Kingdom he envisioned is a collective way of life—a movement—we're supposed to usher in *together*. There is one Spirit, one God, and one faith.[58] While we have a taste of this Kingdom now, we don't see it yet in all its fullness. In this sense, it's both *already* and *not yet* here.

To recap: Jesus' invitation to follow is a call to turn from the way we've been living (repent) and begin living an eternal life (a with-God lifestyle he modeled, available here and now and forevermore).

THE PROBLEM OF SIN: LOSING THE WAY

There's an opposing force to this inbreaking Kingdom: sin. You've probably heard of the problem of sin, and you may or may not fully agree with it. The narrative is that Adam and

Eve—created by God and living in communion with him—
failed morally by eating fruit from the Tree of the Knowledge
of Good and Evil.

Their blunder—not trusting God—had drastic repercussions
for humanity. While before they were naked and unashamed,
after sinning they covered themselves with fig leaves to
hide. This signified a loss of innocence and the entrance of
guilt and shame into the human psyche. God—who saw this
coming from the beginning—kicked them out of the Garden
of Eden, and later sent Jesus as a bridge to cover their (and
our) moral transgressions.

This is *a* Scriptural perspective, but not the *only* one. Viewing
Jesus from only this perspective is like seeing the world in one
color—it's not wrong; there's just *more*. God uses a colorful
palette to paint the portrait of the human condition.

Sin in Hebrew is *chata*, meaning to "lose the way."[59] In Greek,
it's *hamartano*, which means "missing the mark."[60] It's not just
doing morally wrong things; it's a condition of being human.
Our hearts are inclined to drift from God—and in doing so we
"lose the way."

Saying people are sinful isn't any more of a slam than a doctor
telling a patient they have cancer. To say anything less would
be dishonest and unloving.

Whether you believe in the doctrine of sin or not, you can't
deny that if you look around in the world, people have lost
the way and missed the mark. If sin is a disease of the soul,

salvation is the healing balm for our deformed inner being. "Saved" in Greek is *sōzō*—a word which also means "healed."[61] Jesus' saving touch is healing in many ways.

In the account of the woman with the flow of blood who touched Jesus' garment, he turned to her and said:

Take heart, daughter, your faith has healed [sōzō] you.[62]

He healed her *physically, emotionally*, and *eternally*—all at once. Physically, her flow of blood stopped. Emotionally, he washed away the shame of rejection she'd felt from over a decade of ostracism (her flow of blood made her ritually unclean so she was cast out from society). Eternally, he saved her into the Kingdom of God.

All of this healing, according to Jesus, happened *by her faith*.

When Jesus saves, he doesn't just touch one aspect of you—he heals the whole person. Ancient Christians understood this, which is why they called him *the physician of the soul*.[63] He once said:

It's not the healthy who need a doctor, but the sick.[64]

Jesus saw sin as a sickness and himself as the physician. The upshot of all this: his invitation isn't *only* to accept saving grace doctrinally as a covering for your moral transgressions. It's to open your life to his healing—wounds, sin, shame, and all. He's much more than a call to higher moral living.

The Hebrew name for Jesus—*Yeshua*—means "Yahweh [God] is salvation, restoration, and deliverance." Jesus, who repeatedly claimed he was God, believed God's mission for his life was to *save* [sōzō] and restore the world from its sinful state.[65] It's in this sense he said:

I am the way and the truth and the life.[66]

To recap: sin—the internal bent of our soul and our moral transgressions—takes us off *the way*, while Jesus *offers* to return us to it. His claims to be *the way* were so bold they got him murdered. For instance, Jesus said of himself:

Father…you loved me before the creation of the world.[67]

To say he existed at the beginning of it all puts himself on the same level as God. To the woman at the well, he said:

I AM the Messiah![68]

He also forgave sin, which only God can do. To take his claims at face value would mean God walked the earth as a human for over 30 years. How he did it, which is narrated in the scriptural accounts, is *preposterous*. The God of the universe, the Creator of everything, came as a helpless baby to a working-class family in an obscure town.

His stepfather Joseph was a blue-collar worker, and their family lived on the lower end of the middle class.[69] God himself did manual labor, likely as a stonemason, most of his life.[70] Mary and Joseph raised God Jewish. And God practiced his faith regularly.

As C.S. Lewis wrote in Mere Christianity, Jesus' claims to be God either make him a lunatic (delusional), a liar (he made it up), or Lord (everything he said was true).[71] He doesn't leave us any middle ground, or the option of merely being a "good man."

Post-resurrection, Paul claims he appeared to Peter, the 12 disciples, more than 500 others, James, all the apostles, and Paul himself.[72] It's clear Jesus wanted to drive home a point: *Everything I said about myself—resurrection and eternal life—is true.*

His followers became so convinced of his deity they each died horrible deaths rather than renounce his claims. Historian Michael Licona, in *The Resurrection of Jesus: A New Historiographical Approach*, writes of the intense persecution they suffered resulting from their newfound faith in Jesus *after* his resurrection.[73] While in the Gospels they're often depicted as a bumbling, faithless lot, in Acts (post-resurrection) they're emboldened, quick witted (giving speeches on the spot), and full of faith (see Peter praying over the deceased Dorcas in Acts 9 for instance).

What made Peter go from denying Jesus when pressured by a teenage girl to praying to raise the dead and dying upside down on a cross rather than renounce Jesus? A God-inspired spark.

SURRENDERING TO JESUS AS SAVIOR AND TEACHER

One Sunday morning, bitter, tired, and dejected, I went to church with a hollow ache in my chest. Despite being surrounded by people, I was alone, lost in the fog of my own thoughts. I'd isolated and self-medicated for years, keeping everyone an arm's length away. This was my breaking point.

Pastor Mark Daniels—an absolute legend of a human being— preached a simple message that morning. While winding down, he paused, put the notes down, looked into the crowd, and spoke from the heart. His soft-spoken tone became deafening in my ears as the words hit home like punches from a heavyweight fighter:

> *Jesus gave everything for you! God is asking you to give everything in return! Every category of your life. Marriage. Parenting. Relationships. Finances. Career. Hand it over.*

God sparked something in me. I'd been managing *everything* poorly by doing it *my way*. I prayed what is to this day the simplest and most beautiful prayer of my life: *I am yours, God. Have your way. I give up.* A warmth overtook me, like an enveloping hug, and God melted away years of pressure, pain, and bitterness. I sat sobbing for an hour, feeling my frostbitten heart thaw, and a new spring began to bloom inside of me.

His love became real.

Nothing changed on the outside, but internally I knew God was leading me onto a new path and life would never be the same. Words are inadequate to express what it was, but I know—beyond a shadow of a doubt—it was God meeting me where I was and pulling me into the flow of his love. This was my first moment of real surrender.

In the Western Church, Jesus' ability to save is his most highlighted feature in the gospel we hear preached. And certainly, salvation is essential to faith.

> If you declare with your mouth, "Jesus is Lord," and believe in your heart that God raised him from the dead, you will be saved.[74]

David paints a word picture of Jesus' saving power:

> He reached down from on high and took hold of me; he drew me out of deep waters.[75]

Jesus is God's extended hand to save us, which is amazing news! But there's more to him than the ability to save.

Peter, one of Jesus' closest followers, said God made him Messiah [i.e., Savior] and Lord.[76] Over 80 times in the New Testament, we see Jesus' disciples address him as Lord, while they call him Savior 24 times.[77] "Lord" is like "Master," but master meant something different then. When we hear it now, we instinctively think of a cruel and controlling person—like a slave master. But that's not at all what Jesus' early followers meant. In their context, they were addressing him as Master Teacher or Rabbi.

By calling him Savior *and* Lord, they acknowledged him as both Savior and Master Teacher. As Savior, he gave his life as a ransom for us. As Master Teacher, he modeled how to live as an example for us.

In a culture which values independence and self-sufficiency, Jesus as Savior is a hard sell, and Jesus as Savior and Master Teacher is even more challenging. Many see Jesus (and religion) as restrictive and limiting and don't want to be subject to a "lack of freedom." America is, after all, the land of the free and home of the brave.

Entering the Kingdom requires breaking these cultural norms. Surrendering to Jesus and giving him control—considering we've lost *the way* and he is our return—is the most intelligent, freeing, and courageous act we can do. On the contrary, living on our own—independent and self-willed—is not a sign of strength but enslavement. There can be no spark without a yielding of the human spirit to God as the higher power. Make no mistake: Jesus offers to save everyone, but the invitation requires a surrender of *everything* to him as Master Teacher.[78]

That's a scary thought. We live in a world of mistrust, where those in power may abuse it. Surrender offers the opportunity to be hurt and scarred, and you may naturally want to keep control of your life to a certain degree. But how much power do you really have? You don't control God, the weather, opportunities, drunk drivers, cancer, your spouse (if you have one), people, how long you live—the list goes on. The list of things you don't control is substantially longer than the list of those you do.

So why not yield to God, who's already in control? Again, the challenge is that you can't yield a degree of autonomy to a comfortable, culturally created version of Jesus. The ask is *everything* to the Jesus found in Scripture. And Jesus' invitation isn't *only* for a one-time decision. Surrender is the first step into The Way and the daily posture of our hearts as we walk down it.

THE INVITATION TO FOLLOW IS TO BE AN APPRENTICE

Jesus' invitation is simple yet profound:

> *Come to me, all you who are weary and burdened, and I will give you rest. Take my yoke [my teachings and way of life] upon you and learn from me, for I am gentle and humble in heart, and you will find rest for your souls. For my yoke is easy and my burden is light.*[79]

His call—to take on his teachings and way of life—is an invitation to be his *disciple*. Or, as John Mark Comer puts it, to *apprentice* under him.[80] The Greek word for disciple used in the New Testament is *mathētés*, which literally means "learner." "Disciple" appears 261 times in the New Testament, while "Christian" shows up only three.[81] Early followers of Jesus saw themselves as learners (i.e., apprentices, students, and disciples). Jesus commissioned them in the same vein: go and make *apprentices*.[82]

Over time, followers of Jesus adopted the label of "Christians" (i.e., "little Christs"). While there is nothing inherently wrong with the word, what Christian has come to mean (making a decision for Jesus) has been divorced from apprenticeship as practiced by Jesus and his early followers. You can be a Christian (a person who has made a decision for Jesus) and not an apprentice (one who enters a learning relationship under him).

Does the distinction between apprentice and Christian really matter? *Yes.* It entirely misses the point to be a Christian (as defined by culture) and not an apprentice (as defined by Jesus).

This begs the question: what does apprenticeship look like according to Jesus? He paints the picture clearly in the Gospels, summarized by this poignant statement:

> *...A student, when fully trained, will be like the teacher.*[83]

An apprentice, then, is a student faithfully engaged in *training* to become like Jesus. We are to train under our Master Teacher in his way of love, healing, care, serving, protecting, praying, and witnessing (to only name a few things he did). We do this with the aim of living the way Jesus would live if he were in our shoes.

To gain an accurate picture of apprenticeship, we must rely on the cultural context of Jesus' time (which surrounded his invitation to follow him). He doesn't invite us to be learners only in the Western sense of the word, where education happens in a classroom a few times a week through lectures. To be a learner in the Eastern context of discipleship certainly includes education, but the school in which Jesus' apprentices learn is life. There are no breaks, weekends, or holidays.

Apprenticeship, as practiced by the early followers of Jesus, is a 24/7 calling. To be an apprentice is to devote one's entire life to follow in the footsteps of a rabbi. By following Jesus, you become inwardly transformed into a person like him. Again, the aim is to train to become like Jesus internally to the extent that you become a person poised to do what he would do at any point in time.

We not only develop faith *in* Jesus, but the faith *of* Jesus to do the things he did.

Jesus didn't invent the concept of apprenticeship—there were many rabbis in the region with students. During Jesus' time, there was a popular saying: "May you be covered in the dust of your rabbi." This conveys a common understanding about apprenticeship. A students' aim was to follow their teacher so closely they became covered in the dust the rabbi kicked up.

To follow Rabbi Jesus is to follow his *way of life* (i.e., lifestyle). This isn't merely an addition to life as we know it—it's an entirely different one. Accepting his invitation through surrender makes our lives a blank slate and allows Jesus to re-form who we are.

THE PRACTICE OF SELF-DENIAL IN A WORLD OF INDULGENCE

While it only takes a few sentences to write, apprenticeship (inner formation by the Spirit and our effort into a person like Jesus) is the work of a lifetime. Before Jesus, we had our "way" (i.e., the basic framework of life we followed). Like ruts in a road, it guided us to a destination which missed the mark. In the West (an individualized culture), this is often a life oriented around the never-ending pursuit of *enough* (enough things, titles, experiences, and money). This idolization of the American Dream is incompatible with apprenticeship to Jesus. We cannot serve two masters.

When we begin to follow Jesus, he first teaches us to live in self-denial ("deny yourself, pick up your cross, and follow me"[84]). This teaching is a foundational aspect of entering Jesus' way of life. Richard Foster writes about Jesus' call to self-denial. It is:

> ... *simply a way of coming to understand that we do not have to get our own way.*[85]

Jesus doesn't call us to hate ourselves. Picking up your cross is instead about releasing control to God.

It's exhausting to have to get our way all the time. The call to self-denial is Jesus' invitation to be free from the incessant need to be in control. God liberates us—we are no longer enslaved to the idea that we must get what we want at all times—to pursue deeper desires.

At the outset of our apprenticeship to Jesus, we quickly realize we need help if we're going to live this way. Paul, a master follower of Jesus, wrote:

> Those who belong to Jesus have crucified the flesh with its passions and desires.[86]

In other words, following Jesus is returning to a constant internal state of "death to self" (the result of crucifixion).

If you stop and think about the mechanics of crucifixion, you'll see it's not a solo job. Once you nail one hand to the cross, you cannot nail the other. We need help to live in a state of self-denial. To practice self-denial is to be in a constant position of awareness of our dependence on God. Instead of being our own god and meeting all our own needs, we transition to depending on God (and others) to help us live this way.

Let's "flesh" this out more (see what I did there?). The way of the world is giving in to *the flesh*—our surface-level desires—and indulging. Whether it's a Tesla, a hook-up, or fast food, we want it and accordingly feel we must have it. The underlying belief is that indulging every desire immediately leads to satisfaction.

A good example of this is Woody Allen. Allen bought into this narrative when he famously said:

> The heart wants what it wants.[87]

But the heart—separate from Jesus' transformative work—is a bad guide. For instance, Woody gave this quote when explaining why he had an affair with the 27-year-old whom he and his wife had adopted. Allen indulged in his immediate impulses (lust) to the detriment of his deeper desires (a long-lasting marriage).

As we begin to follow Jesus, we develop a new inner framework for the decisions we make. Instead of "What do I want?" we begin to ask different questions like, "What is God's desire in this situation?" and, "Will saying yes to this desire bring me closer to God?" This internal deconstruction of our way for Jesus' way (which happens through the Spirit and constant reflection) isn't possible when we live enslaved to the flesh.

To use another example and not just pick on Allen, I have lusted (which is "to think obsessively about") many things. A lighter example—because lust is not just about sexual desire—is my current obsession with chocolate cake. It's something I want right now. My lust gives me blinders: chocolate cake is all I can see and think about. However, as I begin my walk as an apprentice of Jesus (through a heart posture of surrender and humility), I invite my Teacher to guide my decisions. He reminds me my deeper desire is long-term health so I can be around to watch my children grow old. He widens my view from the immediate desire to the eternal perspective, to help me see how eating this cake now doesn't align with where I want to go.

Abstaining from cake (denying myself what I want now) isn't a practice to make myself miserable. On the contrary, it's a way to love myself in a deeper way. Now of course, it's not a sin to eat chocolate cake (thank God). But you can interchange just about any sin with "chocolate cake."

Before Jesus, you weren't aware of this inner struggle happening between the flesh and spirit, because the flesh drove your actions. But now, as an apprentice, you enter into an inner war zone as you seek to be formed in the way of Jesus. Paul wrote this about the inner struggle he experienced:

> I do not understand what I do.... For I have the desire to do what is good, but I cannot carry it out. For I do not do the good I want to do, but the evil I do not want to do—this I keep on doing.[88]

What a twisted situation we find ourselves in. Pre-Jesus, we idolized living with no boundaries for our desires and went "wherever the wind blows," so to speak. With Jesus, we realize what we actually want is to pursue our deepest desires (which are also God's desires for us). God has given us the desire to be seen, known, and fully loved. But what we do in the flesh runs contrary to what we deeply want.

The way of Jesus is built on uncovering and realizing these deeper eternal desires. To do this, we must embrace Kingdom logic. As we begin to live in this new reality Jesus called the Kingdom, we experience a truth: the things we do produce their opposites. Self-denial—not indulgence—is true freedom. And it's paradoxically by surrender (i.e., submission to Jesus) that we become liberated. While we've only begun to touch the surface of self-denial, it's necessary to frame it in early because it's a foundational piece of "the spark" (and apprenticeship to Jesus).

A LIFESTYLE OF SURRENDER THROUGH A HEART POSTURE OF TRUST

Stephen M.R. Covey, author of *The Speed of Trust*, wrote:

> *Whether you're on a sports team, in an office or a member of a family, if you can't trust one another there's going to be trouble.*[89]

With Jesus, a lifestyle of surrender is only possible with *trust*.

To use a clumsy example, Jesus' invitation to surrender is like being on Michael Jordan's basketball team and having him ask for the ball (your life). After you've come to *believe* he's going to do better with it than you, you may as well pass it. The ego may object, but it's the wise choice.

You *trust* MJ because you *know* he has the skill, pedigree, character, and qualifications to handle it. And if you don't know Jesus (and therefore don't trust him), the first (and continual) priority is getting to know him relationally. You may feel nervous with the first "pass," but over time your fear will subside as you see how Jesus does with your life.

There are many passes—moments of surrender—to make. The Western narrative of surrender is making "one pass to win the game" (i.e., one decision to follow Jesus). Often, we hear romanticized before-and-after testimonies like this: "Before

Jesus, everything was bad. But once I surrendered everything at that altar call back in February of '96, it's been so good." I don't mean to be disparaging because there are powerful moments in the spiritual journey we should celebrate; however, for a person to say they've surrendered once three decades ago is a misunderstanding of Jesus' call to live a surrendered life. He calls us to pick up our cross *daily*, not *once*.

Surrendering once doesn't make problems and deeply ingrained sinful tendencies disappear. Spiritual formation— the inner transformation to become like Jesus—doesn't happen in a lightning-bolt moment. Every day, as part of this journey, we must surrender anew and be continually filled with the Spirit.[90]

When things don't go our way, we're tempted to keep the ball or yank it back. *When* you find surrendering hard—we all have moments—remember *who* you're passing to.

To summarize section two, we face a shared condition of sin (departing from the way), which is much deeper than doing bad things. There is a bent deep inside us to do that which doesn't serve us or honor God. For this condition, we place faith in Jesus—the physician of our souls—to heal us (internally, emotionally, and eternally). Jesus offers rest for our souls, but it comes through a lifestyle—a transformative, relational apprenticeship.

The prerequisite to following Jesus is surrender to him as both Savior and Master Teacher (once initially, and then in every decision and moment after that). This is a high calling, although it is offered to everyone. The aim of following Jesus is to become like him so that through our internal life in the Spirit we can do the things he did.

This apprenticeship will cost you everything, but God will give you immeasurably more in return. If you choose to begin the journey—or recommit to following Jesus in a deeper way—know he is gentle, peaceful, humble, and easy to please.[91]

THREE
STRENGTHENING YOUR FIRE

BUILDING A RULE OF LIFE

God's plan for us is to create a blazing, lifelong, inner fire. Here's the kicker: sparks don't magically become flame. Certain things—ingredients—are necessary for inner fire:

1. *Effort*
2. *God's Spirit*
3. A *Rule of Life*

Effort: Fanning the Flame

As God's Spirit enters the apprentice upon surrender (the spark), we begin the "working out of our faith."[92] While we don't earn God's grace, we're called to participate in our internal transformation. Fanning isn't a haphazard effort—it's doing our very best with what we have to follow Jesus. We cannot simply sit back and expect this process to just happen.

God's Spirit: Empowerment

All the effort in the world can't replace the work of God's Spirit. Whereas a natural fire needs wind, an internal spiritual fire requires the empowerment of the best partner in the world: the Holy Spirit. Notably, wind and Spirit are the same word in Greek. Like the wind, God's Spirit works in invisible ways, doing the heavy lifting of our internal transformation to become more like Jesus. While we receive God's Spirit when we place our trust in Jesus, we must *be continually filled with the Spirit* and *walk in step with the Spirit* to receive his ongoing empowerment.[93]

A Rule of Life: a Framework

In addition to effort and God's Spirit, we need a plan. Another way to put it is that lasting fire requires a *framework* of logs. Picture someone starting a nice campground fire. The wind is blowing, allowing the kindling to catch from a spark—now what's needed? A framework of logs surrounding the kindling. It's the big logs that allow a fire to last through the night.

For our purposes, logs are the things we do (practices) within a larger Rule of Life (more on this in a moment) that allow us to sustain the initial momentum of the Holy Spirit's spark.

All three go together: effort, the Holy Spirit, and a Rule of Life. Together—like intertwined cords forming an unbreakable rope—God works out our inner transformation. To remove even one of these ingredients is to not have a *sustainable* inner fire.

For instance, without effort, God's Spirit and a framework won't do it for us. Jesus values free will and invites all to follow. He does not coerce anyone to walk the narrow road. Effort is not a spiritual gifting, but a choice we make daily in apprenticeship to Jesus.

Without God's Spirit, we can do nothing despite all the effort and plans in the world. And without a plan, our efforts won't have guidance, and the fire never grows.

While each element is incredibly important, Section Three focuses on the "Rule of Life" as it neatly integrates with the other two (effort and God's Spirit).

A Plan to Build a Rule of Life

Let's drill down on the term "Rule of Life." Another word for it is a "framework." Jesus had one. It's a simple yet profound set of practices he structured his life around to keep him abiding (continually connected) with God with a strong inner fire.

Have you heard of the Rule of Life? It's an idea popularized by St. Augustine in AD 397 to help followers of The Way live more intentionally. Specifically, it's a set of rhythms to practice to help you to stay connected to Jesus and produce more fruit.[94]

Think of it like this: Jesus said he is the vine, you are the branch, and God is the gardener.[95] In your spiritual garden, as God works, he can use a *trellis*. The trellis is a framework on which the branches and vine grow. It's a tool to help them grow intertwined and vertically. Why? With a trellis, the branches reach their full potential and produce the most fruit possible. Without it, they do grow—but haphazardly. They can't support the fruit they produce and eventually find themselves on the ground, where there's risk of trampling and disease.

In Greek, the word for Rule—as in Rule of Life—is the same as "trellis."

Simply put, a Rule of Life is a framework by which you live. You may not know it, but you already have a Rule of Life. You've created a framework which guides your daily decisions and rhythms. In fact, your Rule of Life is forming you into a specific kind of person. The problem is, often the Rule of Life we've created isn't *intentional*, so it doesn't form us to be more like Jesus.

The invitation to strengthen your fire requires intentionality to build and practice a new Rule of Life. Like a trellis, it provides structure for your apprenticeship to Jesus. The practices we explore in this section include prayer (solitude, silence, stillness, daily office), Scripture, fasting, and community. These are not an *exhaustive* list of practices—there isn't one. *Anything you do with the intention of aligning yourself to the presence of God can be a practice.*

Of course, some practices are more essential than others. These specific practices appear repeatedly in the life of Jesus and his early followers, although there are certainly more ways to become like him which are highly valuable.

Taking a Training Approach to the Practices

First, the concept of a "practice" is quite simple. It's a *repeated action we intentionally do to become more like Jesus.* Over time, through practice and God's empowerment, our character becomes more like Christ. As a result, we become able to do things we couldn't—or wouldn't—before. To put it another way, we become poised in all situations to do what Jesus would do if he were us.

This concept—training through practice—applies in every area of life. Take sports. If I wanted to run a marathon right now, I could show up in my Nikes, do my best, and perhaps make it a few miles. But there's *no way*—it's a physical impossibility—I could run 26.2 miles today.[96] Even if I intended to do it and tried my absolute best, I simply couldn't.

Dallas Willard writes:

> *A practice is an action we can do now, in order to become able to do what we can't do by direct effort.*[97]

There are a lot of things you and I probably can't do by direct effort *today* (i.e., trying really hard)—run a marathon, play Beethoven's "Ode to Joy" on the piano, dunk a basketball, or conquer our anger with our little children (I hear this is a phenomenon some parents face).

However, a marathon—the thing I can't do today— is possible in the future through training. I'd need to develop an actionable and progressive running plan (e.g., running one mile every day this week, two miles every day the next, and so on). If I made my training program too burdensome at the outset, I'd become exhausted and quit. But if I approached it right, starting with where I'm at, it's conceivable—even likely—that I could run 26.2 miles six months from now.

Athletes inherently understand the value of practice, and they work on skills slowly. There are so many parallels between athletics and the training Jesus invites us into. The Bible provides that Paul:

> *. . . disciplined his body like an athlete, training it to do what it should.*[98]

Steve Kerr, coach of the Golden State Warriors, said the same of Steph Curry:

He loves the process... there's a routine that not only is super-disciplined but it's really enjoyed each day.[99]

Curry practices daily. He does overload training, dribbling two balls at once. In one drill, he wears tinted goggles while dribbling and passing as a trainer throws tennis balls at him. Then, his goggles start flashing, making it harder to see.[100]

He's intensely focused on strengthening the neurological connections between mind and body. Despite not being the tallest, fastest, or most athletic, he's led his team to three championships and made the most three-pointers in NBA history.[101]

But he started with the basics, which evolved over decades into his current training regimen.

Often, what trips us up with the practices is *overtraining.* We overestimate what we can do *today.* It's incredibly important to approach the practices with a *progressive* training mindset. To use the "logs around the fire" analogy, too many logs leave no room for the fire to breathe. Too much of a good thing—taking on too many practices, at too much depth, too quickly—douses your flame as surely as a bucket of water.

Again, the idea behind practicing is simple: do what you're able to do today so you can do what you currently can't do, tomorrow. You eat an elephant one bite at a time (a saying

I've never fully come to peace with). To tackle any task of substance, you break it into bite-sized actions: put on your running shoes, walk a few minutes, run a mile, drink water, and so forth. Becoming like Jesus is no different: practice a minute of silence and stillness, meditate on one verse, fast a meal, and all of a sudden you find yourself *becoming* like your Rabbi.

An aside: in this section, we take time to build a foundation for each practice, which allows new apprentices of Jesus to jump right in without concepts flying over their heads! In each section, there are also ways to more deeply apply each practice. If you feel comfortable with the basics of a particular practice, feel free to skip ahead and explore different aspects and depths of the practice to experiment with. Section Three exists to serve you, so don't be afraid to jump ahead or around!

Every practice won't feel monumental. Sometimes, it feels as if nothing is happening at all. The point is consistency and freeing yourself from the compulsive need to produce and see growth at all times. A ship doesn't "feel" its anchor when directly above it. It's only when it drifts that the tug of the anchor reminds it to return and not go too far. So it is with the practices.

They may go unnoticed to a degree—like an anchor—because they become just what you do. However, when you drift, they will be a helpful vehicle for God to grab your attention and get you back on track. They should not feel like a "burdensome yoke." Instead, they will feel as light as a feather as they become ingrained patterns by which you live.

Of course, unlike a merely physical effort which revolves entirely around our ability, when we invite God's Spirit into our effort, the practices become powerful *vehicles* to connect with God.[102]

The point of a practice isn't the practice—*it's what God does through it.*

The end goal of any practice in a Rule of Life is to be a vehicle—a conduit—through which you and God connect. It's through this connection that God empowers you to be able to do things you never thought possible. Will we become perfect through practice? No. But we will become more like Jesus.

For each practice, there are also tips on how to do it. Scripture gives practically no instruction on the "how" regarding the practices. In the first century (and earlier), the practices were so ingrained in culture that it wasn't necessary to explain how to do them. For instance, because everyone knew how to fast, no author breaks down what to do for the reader. Now, thousands of years later, we no longer share the same cultural knowledge about how to do the practices. As Richard Foster writes in his book, *The Celebration of Discipline*, it's necessary to again teach the mechanics. However, the inner attitude of the heart is far more crucial.[103]

Becoming like Jesus only happens with intentional practice. To put it another way, you won't become like Jesus by accident. No one in human history ever woke up and said: "I'm more Christ-like today. I don't know how—I didn't do anything; it just sort of happened." It's going to take some work. Thankfully, Jesus shows us the way. His rhythms, forming his lifestyle, are the blueprint from which you'll build a new Rule of Life. Let's jump in!

PRACTICE: PRAYER AS CONTINUAL CONVERSATION

Layer One: Exploring Prayer as a Way of Life

If a Rule of Life is like a group of logs around your inner fire, prayer is the *main log*. It's the anchor which keeps you tethered and the rudder through which God steers. It looks like many different things: talking, listening, silence, crying, thinking, yelling—even breathing.

While prayer takes many forms, there is one common denominator, which Pastor Tyler Staton explained masterfully:

> To pray is to willingly put ourselves in the unguarded, exposed position. There is no climb. There is no control. There is no mastery. There is only humility and hope. To pray is to risk being naive, to risk believing, to risk playing the fool.[104]

The point—as we journey through the practice of prayer—isn't to prescribe a one-size-fits-all approach. It's to open you to a *life of prayer* through examining all the ways prayer is life. Once you have a good understanding of how you can pray, the idea is simple: build prayer into your life in a deep and meaningful way.

In any *healthy* relationship, communication is key. It's no different with God. We often approach God—when we pray— by dominating the conversation. We talk *at* him, don't ask questions, and never stop to listen. While there's no such thing as a "bad" prayer, an anchor works best when used correctly. Sure, you can use it as a doorstop, but wouldn't it be better to realize its full potential? The purpose of prayer—like an anchor—is keeping us connected with God.

And let's be real: it can be hard. Talking with an invisible and silent God can feel daunting. Praying to a "Father" can be hard, too, if the word carries baggage. Unanswered or denied prayer can be discouraging. Continued sickness, when we've persistently prayed for health, makes us question whether God hears us at all. There are *all kinds* of challenges when it comes to prayer. Let's start at the beginning.

The same way we create relational depth, connection, and intimacy with others is how we do it with God. He loves a rolling, honest, and continual conversation. This involves listening when he speaks and having the confidence to speak as he listens. It looks like enjoying the silence of each other's company, blabbing on about the things you're excited about, and sharing deep hurts and huge victories with an old friend.

Prayer is an invitation into the ongoing flow of love between Father, Son, and Holy Spirit. Consider these Scriptures about prayer:

People with their minds set on you, you keep completely whole, steady on their feet, because they keep at it and don't quit.[105]

Delight and meditate on his law day and night.[106]

Pray continually.[107]

Remain continually in me.[108]

In Scripture, prayer sounds like a lifestyle. How can we do this—live a life of prayer—when everything requires our attention?

We must be mentally present for work, chores, emails, driving, conversations, changing diapers, and getting groceries. How can we pray throughout the day when life is already so full? Maybe, like me, you start the day with prayer and feel close to God, but by evening, you feel distant, tired, and disconnected.

How can we invite God more and more into our ordinary, mundane, complicated, and messy lives?

Well, it's comforting to know if Jesus says to do something (*remain in him*), we can do it. To put it another way, like a good teacher, he's giving us an assignment a little above our head, but it is possible.

Layer Two: Prayer as a Continual Awareness of the Presence of God

Brother Lawrence was a fascinating example of practicing continual prayer. Living in Paris during the 1600s, he worked in the kitchen of a monastery cleaning pots and pans and repairing sandals. Despite these mundane duties, people always asked him how he was so full of joy. In response, he wrote letters (which comprise a book: *The Practice of the Presence of God*). Here is his philosophy:

> *To be constantly aware of God's presence, we must form the habit of continually talking with Him throughout the day.*

He wrote:

> *...the least little remembrance will always be the most pleasing to Him. One need not cry out loudly; He is nearer to us than we think.[109]*

When asked how to do this, he responded:

> *There is no manner of life in the world more sweet or delicious than a continual conversation with God. They alone can understand it who practice it and savor it.[110]*

He seemed to be saying that words alone can't teach or convey the beauty of a life of prayer—it's something that can only be understood by *practicing*. We don't learn to ride a bike by reading the instruction manual. We simply climb on and start pedaling with wobbly handlebars and pounding heart until, slowly but surely, we experience the joy of the wind in our hair as we fly down the street. In the same sense, we learn how to pray—and the beauty of prayer—by praying.

Continual conversation with God is—at its core—an awareness of God's presence. Jesus is the best example of this kind of life.

He was aware of God because he prayed consistently. He prayed *at all times* of the day. According to Mark:

> *While it was still night, way before dawn, he got up and went out to a secluded spot and prayed.*[111]

Before selecting 12 to apprentice under him, he prayed through the night.[112] He also prayed publicly. When his friend Lazarus died, he prayed in front of a crowd (and God returned Lazarus to life).[113] On another occasion, he prayed in front of tens of thousands, asking God to multiply five loaves and two fish to feed a crowd.[114] After this public prayer, he retreated to a mountainside to pray.[115]

His prayers were sincere and born out of a sense of deep need. When he was tired and hungry, he prayed.[116] Before crucifixion, overwhelmed with sorrow, he prayed. Matthew records his physical posture as he prayed in the Garden of Gethsemane: lying on the ground, face down.[117] Luke added:

> *Sweat like drops of blood poured off his face.*[118]

He prayed three times that night, likely for over an hour each time, asking for the strength to do God's will. If you're catching a theme, it's that he prayed *consistently.*

He lived aware of God. Mark wrote:

*As Jesus was coming up out of the water, he saw heaven being torn open and the Spirit **descending** on [Jesus] like a dove.*[119]

John observed how the Spirit:

*...descended from heaven like a dove and **rested** on him.*[120]

Mark and John show God's Spirit *descending* and *resting* on Jesus—it didn't depart.

In another section of Scripture, Jesus said (before raising Lazarus from the dead): "I know that you [God] always hear me..."[121] The point: Jesus was always talking with God. His connection with the Father, through the Spirit, was continual.

Doves are skittish. They fly off if there's sudden movement or loud noise. To live with God's Spirit, like hosting a dove on our shoulder, is to go through each day with the Spirit in mind. Every action, step, and thought is done with an awareness of God. We live mindful of his presence. Like Jesus, *we* host the Spirit of God. Jesus promised:

...I will send Him (the Holy Spirit) to you [to be in close fellowship with you].[122]

Now, this is a beautiful idea, but it takes a lifetime to master. If your life is anything like mine, you'll put this book down and three minutes later you're back in the chaos of the world. You may even lose your temper once or twice. (I've heard this happens to *other* people…) Continual prayer—abiding—takes *practice*. Our minds naturally wander. God won't shake his head and fly away like a petty dove when you lose mindfulness of him. He'll never leave or abandon you.[123] The idea when you drift from God's presence is to simply become aware you've drifted, chuckle, breathe deeply, and return to an awareness of God. Over time, this becomes second nature, like breathing.

Praying continually does not *require* talking out loud. It can be a three-second pause to invite God into an activity, space, or conversation. It's practicing inviting him into *every moment we're in*. You're doing the dishes *with God*. Exercising *with God*. Meeting *with God*. During a workout, thank him for the ability to move and use your body. Doing the dishes, simply enjoy his presence and reflect on how he cleaned you like you're cleaning the dirty plate of lasagna. Doing yard work? Reflect on the deeply rooted weeds he's pulled out of your life. It sounds funny, but you get the picture.

Simply put, prayer is life with God, which is the most delightful way to experience each day.

Sidebar on Layer Two: God Also Communicates through Dreams and Visions

God can talk with us however he wants, much like a parent can choose the way to communicate with a child. Sometimes parents use quiet voices (when the children listen); other times, a louder voice is needed (when one needs to get the attention of a child). We'll take a moment here, in our conversation about prayer as continual communication, to talk about other ways God communicates with us.

A vision or dream can be from God. When received and interpreted, either can be a monumental occasion in one's faith journey. It's only in the last several centuries we've begun to disregard dreams as nothing more than Freudian lapses into the subconscious. In Scripture, we see several instances of God sending dreams, visions, and trances to people. In a dream, God directed Paul to go to Macedonia. He gave Joseph a vision for his future. And in a trance during a noon-hour prayer session, God asked Peter to let go of his ethnic prejudices and share the gospel with non-Jews. Certainly, God can do the same now as he did then.

However, let's explore why God may communicate via dream or vision (methods other than continual conversation). Primarily, it's a way to get our attention, much like a parent using a different tone of voice with a child. Dallas Willard observed God didn't need to get Jesus' attention via vision or dream because he was already paying attention through continual conversation (i.e., abiding).[124] Jesus was "on the line," so to speak. In another portion of Scripture, God spoke with Moses face-to-face, but to Miriam and Aaron (prophets) via visions and dreams.[125] Why?

The principle is simple: if you're closer to God, the communication is clearer and there is less need for dreams, visions, and altered states of reality for God to get your attention. Dreams and visions require interpretation. God's still small voice—spoken directly to us through continual communication—doesn't. To *constantly* rely on things other than continual communion with God as the *primary* means of hearing him is problematic (this can happen individually and in a larger church group). The mature follower knows and primarily listens for the gentle and continual voice of the Shepherd.

While we shouldn't despise dreams and visions, we also must avoid elevating them as a special mode of communication reserved for the "spiritual elite." More could be said on the spiritual abuse justified because a leader "had a vision from God," but we have perhaps stirred the pot enough for you to get the picture. If Jesus spoke to our day and age, I believe he'd return us to John 10 and 15 and this simple truth:

> *My sheep listen to my voice; I know them, and they follow me."*[126]

Sidebar on Layer Two: How Habitual Sin Disrupts Connection with God

Another pertinent question surrounding prayer is whether we can be in continual communication with God if we're in *habitual* sin. Habitual sin isn't a mistake or failure, it's a willful lifestyle of intentional and unrepentant wrongdoing toward God and others. One of Jesus' closest followers, John, wrote:

> *If we claim to have fellowship with him yet walk in the darkness, we lie and do not live out the truth.*[127]

While we all sin, walking in the darkness is choosing not to walk with God (who is light).

To return to the dove analogy, habitual sin is like willfully shooing the dove off your shoulder every time it tries to land. In this scenario, his Spirit will depart. King Saul disobeyed God, sought to honor himself, and lived in a rebellious way. God's Spirit and anointing left as a result.[128] Saul *repeatedly* refused to confess his wrongdoing, pray for forgiveness, and bring himself back to God. In this sense, he refused to host God's Spirit, so God simply granted his desire to be without him.

Layer Three: Prayer as Intentional Time with God

Henri Nouwen—priest, professor, writer, and theologian—once asked Mother Teresa for advice. She responded:

> *Spend one hour each day in adoration of your Lord and never do anything you know is wrong. Follow this, and you'll be fine.*[129]

Her answer is beautifully simple and hints at an essential practice in a life of prayer: *intentional time with God.*

Developing a Vision of Intentional Time with God

Set times of intentional prayer complement continual conversation, like a date night complements regular conversation with a spouse. We know intentional time with God is good but fall short in building it into our schedule and sticking with it. This isn't because we're bad people; instead, we don't have a compelling vision of what our life could look like through this practice.

The parallel examples are endless, but let's use exercise. We don't fail to work out simply because we don't do it. We fail because we don't have a compelling vision of what life would be like if we did. We don't know—because we're so used to the status quo—just how great life would be if we exercised. Without a compelling vision driving our behavior, when it gets hard, we'll quit.

C.S. Lewis wrote on our lack of vision:

> *Indeed, if we consider the unblushing promises of reward and the staggering nature of the rewards promised in the Gospels, it would seem that Our Lord finds our desires not too strong, but too weak. We are half-hearted creatures, fooling about with drink and sex and ambition when infinite joy is offered us, like an ignorant child who wants to go on making mud pies in a slum because he cannot imagine what is meant by the offer of a holiday at the sea. We are far too easily pleased.*[130]

Before we get into the practicalities, let's entertain a question: what would life be like if you started each day with an hour of prayer? How do you think you'd "be" during the day if you spent an hour with God first thing in the morning? It's only through the development of a compelling vision that intentional time with God becomes a reality.

Implementing the Vision of Intentional Time with God

Nature abhors a vacuum.

Even with a vision, without a plan you'll *never* get consistent quiet time with God. This may feel overwhelming, but remember: you can experiment with this practice to find what works for you. For me, I know that I am a much more loving, gracious, and kind person when I've started my day with time alone with God and have regular check-ins with him throughout the day. I know this because on the days I haven't, I've observed myself being such a grouch! We'll get to the practical steps later, but stay with this subject as we build to what it can look like for you.

Time-blocking is the practice of pre-dedicating specific blocks of time to meet with God. Cal Newport, author of *Deep Work*, explains that time-blocking *works* (although he is speaking to a different audience, his insights are valuable for the purposes of this book).[131] In the marketplace, a 40-hour time-blocked workweek produces the same output as a 60+ hour workweek. We can draw a principle from Newport's research: planning our day with intention (in this case, to be with God) is a wise way to steward our time. And it's bigger than merely becoming more productive—it's refreshing for our souls.

Time at Jesus' feet is non-negotiable for the committed apprentice.

A universal relational truth: *there cannot be relational depth without time spent.*

You will develop intimacy with God if you make the time. Can you think of a healthy married couple you know who doesn't spend intentional time together?

Intentional time with God is undistracted and unhurried, solely focused on him. When Jesus was with his apprentices

Mary and Martha, Martha rushed around while Mary sat at his feet, listening. Jesus said being with him was:

> ... the better thing that wouldn't be taken away from her.[132]

He didn't say Martha was *wrong* for working, but that Mary prioritized "better" by first being with him.

In an article titled "If I Could Start All Over," John Piper reflects on prioritizing time with God. He says:

> Read your Bible every day. Every day of your life—no exceptions. Never say, "I'll read it if I have time." If you have time for breakfast, you have time for your Bible. Skip breakfast.[133]

We can apply his statement to time with God in general. The hard truth is we make time for what's most important to us.

It means a great deal to God to spend time with you. Every time you connect with him, he's listening joyfully.

> The eyes of the Lord are on the righteous and his ears are attentive to their prayer...[134]

As an apprentice of Jesus, you are righteous in God's eyes and have his undivided attention. Unlike humans with limited mental capacity, God is always thinking about you. C.S. Lewis put it like this:

> Almost certainly God is not in time. His life does not consist of moments one following another... Ten-thirty—and every other

moment from the beginning of the world—is always Present for Him. If you like to put it this way, He has all eternity in which to listen to the split second of prayer put up by a pilot as his plane crashes in flames.[135]

Even if you feel you can only offer him a moment, know that he is pleased and simply wants your heart to be well. He also knows that time with him is exactly what produces that well-spring of heart-health in your life. You have his ear for all eternity.

At the end of the section on prayer, we discuss how to build intentional time with God into your life. Before that, let's examine additional layers to intentional time with God: silence, solitude, and stillness.

PRACTICE: PRAYER AS BEING WITH GOD

Layer Four: Listening Prayer

Listening while praying seems like a paradox because we associate prayer with talking. And while a large part of prayer is moving our lips, we often neglect the "listening" aspect. As the saying goes: "You can't listen if you're talking."

Jesus listened to God by being silent, alone, and still. The impact of these practices done together is profound. Do you need to sell all your belongings and live in a monastery to have this sort of life? Not at all! It's available here and now for regular people like you and me, but we must plan and work to create a contemplative life. Like Jesus, we can implement these patterns into our hurried lives to help us slow down and walk with God, not ahead of him.

Prayer is a necessity, like inhaling deeply before speaking. Jesus' life rhythm was inhaling (*being with* God) before exhaling (*doing for* God). Culture teaches us to rest from work (i.e., rest is recovering from work, for the purpose of recharging to work again). We rest from work on evenings, weekends, and vacations only to return refreshed to work. Jesus reversed this order: he worked from a place of rest.

For him, walking and being in nature were deep breaths for his soul. He constantly withdrew to hills, mountains, seashores, and parks like the Garden of Gethsemane. [136] He was onto something through this rhythm of mobile meditation. Retreating to nature, God's creation, is *so* good for humans (neurologically and physiologically).

The demands on Jesus' time were overwhelming. So many people wanted a piece of him. Our lives feel the same. There is always more work to be done (i.e., *exhaling*). We live in a culture of performance, production, noise, and bustling activity. If this is all we do, we find ourselves bone-dry on the inside. Culture has taught us how to *do*. It's the *inhaling*—the filling of the inner self with fresh air—we must learn. In the words of philosopher Blaise Pascal:

All of humanity's problems stem from man's inability to sit quietly in a room alone.[137]

Layer Five: Silent Prayer

When Rosie and I started dating, we couldn't stop talking to and about each other. We were euphoric about this new love (and probably pretty annoying). Every moment together was filled with noise, laughter, and conversation. Underneath this honeymoon season of love was an insecurity: we weren't comfortable with silence. We felt a need to entertain each other through humor, stories, and conversation. It felt uneasy to simply *be* together. Over 15 years of dating and marriage, we've become more comfortable with silence. We enjoy pauses, taking in the sunset, and walks in which we simply *are* with each other. Of course we still talk, but it's not because we fear silence.

Author and Pastor Rich Villodas writes:

The more familiar you are with someone, the more comfortable you are being silent in their presence.[138]

This is also true with God. Oftentimes, because we're unfamiliar with him, we feel a need to entertain him with constant noise. When we make time to be with God, he gently reminds us we can relax and simply *be* with him.

The prophet Elijah learned of the power of God's healing presence by slowing down to *be* with him on a quiet mountain. Here's the story: After Elijah secured a public victory for God, Queen Jezebel threatened to kill him. He suffered a nervous breakdown and fled to Mount Horeb (requiring a *long* journey through the desert). During the trip, he became despondent. He stopped, lay down under a broom bush, and wrote the equivalent of a suicide note: "I want to die!" His soul was in deep agony.

Exhausted, he slept. An angel woke him, encouraging him to eat (God provided bread and water). He ate, slept, and awoke, and God encouraged him to drink and eat (again). God strengthened him for the rest of the journey. *Finally,* he reached the sacred mountain. When he arrived, he found a cave and slept again. There were no cheering crowds or Jezebel—it must have been starkly quiet. Then there were moments of high velocity wind, an earthquake, and a raging fire that eventually dissipated.

Finally, as Elijah sat in the silence, he heard God's *soft voice* encouraging him to go on.[139] The stress in his mind and soul disappeared as he sat still and began to dialogue with God in the stillness. This is an amazing picture of how we naturally come to a place of conversation with God.

It's okay—even spiritual—to nap, eat, recover, complain, and then start talking. God is in it all.

The prophet Isaiah wrote:

> *In quietness and trust is your strength.*[140]

Silence is strength. But it's more than ceasing to speak (or napping). It's curating a space free from distraction (noise, words, mental chatter, and music) to be with God. These spaces—whether 10 minutes or a weekend retreat—are sacred. If you're a parent, extrovert, phone owner, or member of society, this will be challenging. But it's possible—to different degrees—for everyone to do it.

Sometimes we avoid listening to God because we're afraid of what he'll say. Or, we feel we don't hear him at all. But—as God showed Elijah—he is a place of refuge and rest. He's life-giving. Like a dry sponge, we don't need to work to soak in his presence. We simply sit with him and be.

We must fight for silence because we live amid the constant drone of noise pollution. Nothing against sound—we're told in the Psalms:

> Shout for joy to the Lord, all the earth,
> Burst into jubilant song with music.[141]

But there's a rhythm we've lost between silence and noise.

As we quiet ourselves, God works. He turns raging inner storms into tranquil rivers. He orients us back to his way. Often this is beyond our understanding. The Spirit in us communicates with God in ways *deeper than words*.[142] Silence fosters this deep spirit-to-spirit connection. That's all it is.

Layer Six: Praying Alone (Solitude)

Henri Nouwen wrote:

> Solitude is the furnace of transformation.[143]

In *Reaching Out: The Three Movements of the Spiritual Life,* he continued:

> *To live a spiritual life we must first find the courage to enter into the desert of our loneliness and to change it by gentle and persistent efforts into a garden of solitude.*[144]

God uses solitude to encounter and transform us. And Rabbi Jesus withdrew *as often as possible* to secluded places to pray.[145]

This kind of prayer requires being alone, away from other people. Like silence, it's entering an introspective space (looking inward) to hear God's voice. Only by throwing metal into a furnace—engulfing it in extreme heat—does its shape become malleable and moldable. This is the picture of God's work through solitude. He melts, molds, and changes us as we seek him. He helps us get in touch with who we really are.

The practice of withdrawal is crucial for personal development. Solitude—as Nouwen said—at first feels like a "desert of loneliness." It's hard to be alone, but we must pry ourselves away from the compulsion to constantly be around noise and people. Over time, this practice turns from a desert into a garden, the place we feel most alive.

To practice solitude is to follow the footsteps of Jesus, who taught:

> *When you pray, go into your closet and shut the door and pray to your Father who is in secret.*[146]

In his time, the "closet" was a small, dark storage room in the middle of the house. Jesus isn't saying to spend mornings in your pantry, but simply that prayer is a practice which hinges on secrecy. There must be times when it's just us and God.

Solitude—like prayer—requires *practice*. It's not a spiritual gift anyone is born with. We get better at it by doing it. We need wisdom to discern *how* to pursue alone time with God in each season of life. While how we practice solitude may vary, we can all make space daily, weekly, monthly, and yearly for time alone with God.

Layer Seven: Praying in Stillness

When we're hurt or sick, the doctor's advice is usually the same: lie down and rest. Jesus—the physician of our souls—gives the same prescription for our inner life. He says *being still restores the soul*.[147] Stillness is ceasing to "do" and choosing to "be" with God. It's more than a physical posture; it's an internal decision to rest in God.

Here is what Scripture says about stillness:

Be still before the Lord and wait patiently for him.[148]

Be still and know that I am God.[149]

Be still and *wait*. Be still and *know*. Waiting and knowing aren't things we "do"—they are heart postures. My friend

Walter shared a helpful insight into "being" and "doing." Jesus' last command was to "do" (*go* and make disciples). However, his last words were to "be" (*wait* for the Holy Spirit). So which is it, *do* or *be*? Both, in rhythm. We're to *be* (waiting for God's Spirit) before we *do* (going and making disciples).

We work from a place of stillness and rest.

Do you remember the last time you were truly still and at rest before God? Bringing our inner being to stillness, when we're used to running 100 miles an hour, feels uneasy. We feel guilty about not worshiping at the altar of productivity.

I recently took a four-day retreat to a prayer cabin (no Wi-Fi or phone). The first thing I did was read the guest book cover to cover and clean the windows. I was *fidgety*. It took two days to get the "doing" and "producing" out of my system. It takes time to slow down and still ourselves before God. The last two days were serene. I became free to "be" and enjoy things (long walks on the beach without a journal for instance). Stillness is challenging, whether for 10 minutes or four days. But it's highly rewarding beyond words.

God quiets inner turmoil, slows our breathing, and allows us to take in his presence. He re-orients us to his will as we center ourselves on him. Throughout Scripture, people hear God when they're still and mindful, not running around like chickens with their head cut off. Revelation happens in stillness. Samuel was still in the Temple when he heard God's call.[150] Peter was still on the rooftop when God told him to preach to the Gentiles. Jesus was still in the Garden of Gethsemane when God strengthened him for the ordeal ahead.

Envision this: you're seated before the Lord, eyes closed, breathing through your nose. You whisper, "Come, Holy Spirit," and wait. A calm washes over you like waves, God's presence meeting you in the quiet, calming the restless worries of your mind. Consider the transformative power of daily moments of quietude, and how utterly different your life could become by choosing to be still.

Where will you be still?

PRACTICE: PRAYER AS DAILY OFFICE

Building on the idea of intentional time with God through silence, solitude, and stillness, an accompanying practice is the *daily office*. In the Hebrew and early Christian traditions there was a daily prayer rhythm of seeking God at set times of the day (morning, midday, and evening). St. Benedict named the existing practice the "daily office."

People used to regularly pray at certain times: day and night (Psalm 92v2), in the early morning (Psalm 130v6), three times a day (Psalm 55v17), and seven times a day (Psalm 119v164–165).

Praying three times a day has been a foundational practice for thousands of years, although it's rare now. Daniel, during Israel's exile, worked high up for a foreign government (Babylon). Although Babylon tried to assimilate him into their world—even giving him a new name—he resisted through daily set times of prayer.[151]

Eventually, the king decreed no one could pray to anyone but him for 30 days. What did Daniel do?

> When Daniel learned that the decree had been signed and posted, he continued to pray just as he had always done. His house had windows in the upstairs that opened toward Jerusalem. Three times a day he knelt there in prayer, thanking and praising his God.[152]

Although the penalty was death, Daniel was willing to die rather than stop.

David, God's anointed King, also prayed three times a day. He wrote:

> I will call to God for help, and the LORD will save me. I speak to God morning, noon, and night. I tell him what upsets me, and he listens to me![153]

God called David a man after his own heart, not because David was perfect, but because he always returned to him in prayer.

Early followers of The Way prayed at set times as well. For instance, Peter prayed at 9:00 AM, 12:00 PM, and 3:00 PM.[154]

When Peter had the vision which led him to Cornelius' house (and inviting non-Jewish people into The Way—a big deal), it was during a noon prayer session.[155]

However, over hundreds of years, the practice of set prayer became *complicated*. Three set times of prayer turned into seven, each with its own emphasis and specific requirements.[156] In turn, it appears ordinary, working-class people stopped doing it because it became impractical. It became a practice for the "spiritual elite."

If simplified, everyone can practice the daily office. In *Emotionally Healthy Spirituality*, pastor and author Pete Scazzero provides six reasons to build daily office into our Rule of Life:

It gives our day structure.
It's beautiful (the Psalms are poetic and help us express feelings we find hard to say).
It's reorients us to truth—to who God is.
It unites us as we join other followers in set times of prayer.
It makes us content as we remember we have enough in God.
It's formative, as Scripture influences our feelings, as opposed to feelings driving our lives.[157]

Daily office typically involves praying a Psalm. Notably, Jesus' early followers prayed the Psalms together.[158] The Psalms are raw. They are prayers of deep lament, anger, and disappointment. Instead of burying hard feelings and giving God surface-level conversation, the Psalms draw us into deeper waters, guiding us to confront and open up about our real feelings: anger, fear, hurt, sadness, bitterness, envy, melancholy, joy, and exuberance.

Read Psalm 88 for instance—it's a deep cry from the Psalmist with no real answer—it's just how he feels. As we engage, we find we are welcoming God into our wounds, not keeping him an arm's length away. We remember to praise, thank, and trust him in the midst of not knowing how it will all turn out.

Daily office helps us stay aware of God's presence throughout the day. Here is a simple version of what a set time of prayer could look like. Begin with a moment of silence, breathing deeply and welcoming the Holy Spirit. ("Come, Holy Spirit.") Pray a Psalm (read it out loud to God, as if it were you saying the words). Let the Holy Spirit guide you in prayer (which may be directed to a particular area based on something God placed on your heart through the Psalm). Say a guided prayer (such as the Lord's Prayer or Psalm 23).

You can pick a theme for each session (morning, afternoon, evening). For instance, in the morning, many focus on being with God through praying the Lord's Prayer (more on this later). In the afternoon, pray the same Psalm and intercede for one other person. I keep index cards at my desk for each day of the week with a few names on each. In the evening, pray reflectively (reflect on when you felt closest to God, furthest from God, and one prayer you have for tomorrow).

Putting It All Together: Intentional Prayer, Silence, Solitude, Stillness, and Daily Office

By now, we've painted a broad picture of a life of prayer: continual conversation and intentional times to be with God. Our internal posture is one of silence, solitude, and stillness. We may choose to implement the daily office to help us actualize our intentions and vision.

Let's learn by doing. Set the book down and find a quiet place. Spend 180 seconds on your knees or simply seated—palms up, feet uncrossed—with your eyes closed. Breathe deeply and don't set a timer. When your mind wanders, return to an anchoring thought: "The Lord is my Shepherd."

Go!

Welcome back. How was it? What did you feel? What did you observe about yourself? The big idea is to spend every day with Jesus, which takes planning (just like you'd plan to spend a day with a friend from out of town).

Start with the morning. This could be planning to start the day with a quiet walk, 60 seconds of silence, solitude, and stillness, followed by coffee, journaling, and reading Scripture. Whatever your plan is, the point is to have one. If you have a family, factor in what time you need to wake up (i.e., what time you need to go to bed to wake up at that time). I've had many mornings of sleeping in and trying to "cram" time with Jesus while the kids are up, and it isn't fair to anyone. Getting rest the prior evening is essential. In the afternoon, you could plan a set time to "retreat" and pray for a few minutes. And in the evening, you could find a window of time to reflect on the day you've just had.

Weekly, you can practice one day (24 consecutive hours) of intentional rest (called the Sabbath). On this day, choose to not do any paid or unpaid "work." Rest, enjoy what God has given, and take it easy. Our family takes a day of rest from Friday evening to Saturday evening. I find it relaxing to unplug from technology (my phone goes in a drawer), take a long walk, play basketball, and spend time with our family. If we watch a movie, we'll do it together. This is restful for my soul and leaves me ready for the next week.

Three to four times a year (quarterly), you can plan a personal retreat (even if only for three hours). This could be as simple as spending the morning in a quiet park or library to review and evaluate where you are. How are the practices going? Are you becoming more like Jesus? Where do you feel God putting his finger on you to grow? Are you achieving your life goals and calling? What do you need to do differently? What have you been saying yes to that you should say no to? These are all great questions to ask to help you lift your head out of the daily grind.

Annually, you could plan a longer retreat. My wife and I give each other one vacation a year to do what we want. She goes on a cruise with some girlfriends, while I enjoy a personal prayer retreat (as mentioned earlier). It's not easy to get away, especially from four young kids and a full-time job, but it is essential to my apprenticeship to Jesus.

The point is to build a Rule of Life to help you to live at a slower, mindful, and calm pace. Take a progressive approach if this is new, and set reasonable goals you can stick with on your worst day. When you miss, get back up and try again.

As you engage in practicing a life of prayer, you'll find your mind begins to slow down and rest, and the connection with God becomes incredibly life-giving. You may notice your interactions with people changing as well.

We've covered continual prayer, intentional time with God, listening prayer, and daily office. Now we're going to turn to liturgical prayer (praying Jesus' model prayer).

PRACTICE: PRAYER AS LITURGY FROM OUR LIPS

Ask and it will be given to you; seek and you will find; knock and the door will be opened to you – Jesus, Matthew 7v7-8 (NIV)

Do you ever find it hard to *start* talking with God? What are you supposed to say? Do you just…begin? Some prayer is free-flowing and conversational. But Jesus also provided a framework—like a trellis—to help guide our conversations with God. This section explores how we can pray using his "model prayer," often called the Lord's Prayer.

Jesus' Model Prayer

Prayer was not a new concept to Jesus' apprentices. They were all Jewish, and praying was a central part of their culture and upbringing. But something about watching their new Rabbi pray was electric. He prayed *differently*. So, they asked him how to pray, and he taught them.

Jesus' prayer serves as a model for how to approach God. Many shy away from guided prayer (which is a form of liturgy) and prefer to pray in a free-flowing way. Only 20 percent of modern churchgoers pray by repeating a set prayer.[159] But when his disciples asked how to pray, Jesus didn't respond: *Say anything you want in whatever order you want.*

Guided prayer is a freeing, beautiful, and life-giving practice. Talking with God shouldn't be dreaded; it can be the space in which we feel most vibrant, alive, and authentic. We can't expect an *expansive* life and pray an inch *deep*. Guided prayer is a key way to deepen our prayer life.

Here is Jesus' model prayer:

> *Our Father in heaven, hallowed be your name, your kingdom come, your will be done on earth as it is in heaven. Give us today our daily bread. And forgive us our debts, as we also have forgiven our debtors. And lead us not into temptation, but deliver us from the evil one.*[160]

People have devoted entire books to analyzing these 53 words. At first glance, the prayer seems to contain many different ideas, but there's a progression and beauty in its cadence.

Ordering: Begin with God

Jesus begins the prayer focusing on God (*Our Father in heaven, hallowed be your name, your kingdom come, your will be done on earth as it is in heaven*). Then, the prayer pivots to our needs (*Give us today our daily bread. And forgive us our debts, as we also have forgiven our debtors. And lead us not into temptation, but deliver us from the evil one*). This order is intentional. Jesus teaches us to begin with praise before jumping into requests.

Language: We're in This Together

Along with order, the wording throughout the prayer is communal. The speaker is directed to pray using *our* and *us*, not *me* and *my*. Following Jesus is a team sport. It's not just *me* praying; it's *we*. Through communal language, Jesus reminds us we're praying *with* other apprentices around the world.

Our

As we begin the prayer with **Our** *Father*, we remember we have brothers and sisters, fathers and mothers, and sons and daughters in the family of faith. In a world of disunity, *Our Father* draws us to oneness as a body of believers. It reorients us from an individualistic faith to a communal pilgrimage.

Father

Calling God *Father* makes the heart soar. Before Jesus, God wasn't *Father*. *Father* signifies a new era, an intimate shift from the more formal names for God used before Jesus. Jesus changes how we address God, from "Sir" to "Papa." *Father* reminds us God is close, personal, and intimate. *Father* evokes in us that we are children. In this sense, as we pray *Our Father,* we allow ourselves to relax into childlikeness in God's arms. Unlike the rest of the day, when we wear the hats of spouse, parent, employee, and so forth, as we pray, we're simply son or daughter.

In heaven

As we speak these words, our minds center on God, our collective Father, existing *in heaven.* When we think about heaven, we typically picture a place far away in the sky, a sort of cloud city. That's not at all what heaven means in the New Testament, or what Jesus was conveying here. If we look to the Greek, heaven is plural, so a more literal translation is: "Our Father in the heavens."

"Heavens" simply means the air or sky. With this understanding, we correctly frame what Jesus said to be: "Our Father in the air all around us." Jesus isn't telling us to pray as if God is far; rather, he reminds us God is as near as the very breath in our lungs. He's as close as the air all around us. And like air, he never ceases to be near.

This is a truth we recall by pausing after the first four words to take a deep breath. *Our Father in Heaven.* Breathe. As you inhale deeply, remember that like air, God is near.

Our Father in heaven reminds us to start by being with God, who is near. We don't begin our time with requests ("God, can you…God, I need you to…"). Often, we're tempted to run past being with *Our Father in the air all around us* and rattle off a list of things we want him to do. Our kids do this when they visit their grandparents (who habitually give them treats). They rush in the door and the first words are: "What did you get me?" I remind them it's important to give Papa and Grandma a big hug and say "hi." Yes, enjoy the treats as they come (Papa and Grandma won't forget), but treat them as grandparents you love, not an ATM. It's the same with God.

Hallowed be your name.

Hallow: to regard or treat as holy. We don't *make* God holy; we treat him like he is. God is *Our Father*, but he's also *Our King*. It's a seeming paradox: on one hand we can be as comfortable as a child in his arms, and on the other, we shouldn't get too flippant with the King of Kings. The first eight words of Jesus' model prayer acknowledge God's beautiful duality: *intimate Father* and *Holy King*.

Your Kingdom come.

God, lift our eyes from the physical and temporal to the spiritual and eternal. Remind us to seek your Kingdom and righteousness first, and you'll care for our daily needs.[161] When we pray, our spirit seeks God's Kingdom and righteousness. Paul wrote:

> *We fix our eyes not on what is seen, but on what is unseen, since what is seen is temporary, but what is unseen is eternal.*[162]

We fix our eyes on the Kingdom which is within us and is to come.

Your will be done on earth as it is in heaven.

The focus shifts from *God and who we are* to *his work and what we need to do*. Praying for God's will to be done isn't a passive request—as if there's someone else to do it. We say these words to remember we're God's partners on earth. *We're the ones who do his will here.* We're active participants who see opportunities each day to bring his plan closer to fruition. St. Augustine said:

> *Without God, we cannot. Without us, God will not.*[163]

For whatever reason, the God of the universe chooses to work with us to accomplish his will.

Are we truly praying for God's will to be done on earth or our own? The way to determine the answer is simple. If God answered our prayers *right now*, what would change? Would only our lives improve, or would God's will be done on earth as it is in heaven? If our answered prayers would only impact our life, we're praying too small. We seem inclined, as Paul observed, to ask for what's best for ourselves instead of what's most important to Jesus.[164]

Over time, God aligns *our wants* with *his*. He encourages us to pray scary, world-changing prayers. A bold prayer burns as many calories as a boring one. Bold prayers please God because they acknowledge who he is: a big God. Our requests reflect how we see God. If my kids begged me for pennies, I'd be hurt. At times, we only ask God for scraps when he has so much more to give. God wants us to ask him for everything he can do.

We are confident he hears us whenever we ask for anything that pleases him. And since we know he hears us when we make our requests, we also know that he will give us what we ask for.[165]

Pray big, not boring.

Give us today our daily bread.

God, please meet our basic needs and remind us you care for us. We must collect God's provision of manna daily—we cannot eat the manna of yesterday. Thanking God for what he provides makes us appreciate the little things we often take for granted—food, water, and shelter, for instance. And it reminds us we are utterly dependent on him.

Forgive us as we forgive others.

God has forgiven us through Jesus, yet we still fall short. Remembering *our need* for forgiveness keeps us humble before God and empathetic with others. As God's grace sinks into our bones, he transforms us into forgiving, compassionate, and kind people.[166]

We're least compassionate with others when we *forget* our need for God's forgiveness. Therefore, to train to be a loving and forgiving disciple of Jesus, practice *confessing*. Daily confession to God keeps our hearts healthy. Listen to what David wrote about the physical toll of unconfessed sin:

When I kept silent, my bones wasted away through my groaning all day long. For day and night, your hand was heavy on me; my strength was sapped, as in the heat of summer. Then I acknowledged my sin to you and did not cover up my iniquity. I said, "I will confess my transgressions to the Lord." And you forgave the guilt of my sin.[167]

Holding onto unforgiveness produces resentment, bitterness, and frustration. Refusing to forgive is like setting yourself on fire and hoping the other person dies of smoke inhalation. Forgiveness releases the poison of bitterness which takes root when we hold on to an offense.

It can be hard to find the words to ask for forgiveness and to forgive others. Here is a guided prayer of confession and forgiveness:

Most merciful God, we confess that we have sinned against you in thought, word, and deed, by what we have done, and by what we have left undone. We have not loved you with our whole heart; we have not loved our neighbors as ourselves. We are truly sorry and we humbly repent. For the sake of your Son Jesus Christ, have mercy on us and forgive us; that we may delight in your will, and walk in your ways, to the glory of your Name. Amen.

If you feel unable to forgive, remember the Holy Spirit is a helper who provides the strength we need. God is the one who works in us, giving us the ability to fulfill his good purpose. Despite our natural inclination to react negatively toward those who wrong us, Peter reminds us we must bless those who hurt us and not retaliate in kind.[168] This can only be achieved through opening ourselves to God's immeasurable power.

Lead us not into temptation but deliver us from evil.

Apprentices to Jesus aren't exempt from temptation. God allows tests to refine our character and strengthen our dependence on him. Seen in this light, temptations are opportunities to grow. If God removed them altogether, we'd remain untested and immature.

Instead, daily we remember not to be naive as we live in the world. Temptation is a reality of life. It's when we act on these desires that we sin, which produces death.[169]

Temptation isn't sin.

Martin Luther once said tempting thoughts are like birds landing on our head. We don't control the birds (every thought which comes to mind) but can prevent them from building a nest in our hair (fixating on tempting thoughts). In other words, when tempting thoughts come, we'd do well to be mindful of our inner state, not fantasize about the temptation, and redirect our mind to God.

As Jesus fasted in the desert for 40 days, the enemy tempted him three times. He fought back by quoting memorized Scripture. Training to be able to respond like Jesus to temptation is the practice of thought redirection. When tempted, we shift our focus to God by *replacing lies and deception with the truth.*

Typically, we try to fight temptation by focusing on not sinning. It's a losing strategy to focus on avoiding a negative. To continually repeat the thought *I'm not going to sin* is the same as a coach telling a team, *Just don't lose this game.* This keeps the mind focused on the temptation, much like when you're told not to think about a pink elephant, that's exactly what you'll think of.

The better practice is acknowledging the thought and redirecting: "*I'm feeling tempted by [x]. I choose at this moment to focus on the truth: [Scripture].*"

In every situation, God provides an "escape hatch." Paul wrote,

> …*God is faithful; he will not let you be tempted beyond what you can bear. But when you are tempted, he will also provide a way out so that you can endure it.*[170]

What's the way out? It can be practicing thought redirection.

It can also be the wisdom to avoid tempting situations. We're to make ourselves invisible to sin and *flee from it.*[171] It's foolish to willingly be in situations that test our limited willpower. Like a muscle, our ability to make good decisions becomes fatigued as we exercise it throughout the day. That's why we make worse decisions at the end of the day than the beginning.

We eat the worst, indulge the most, and say the things we wish we hadn't when we lack the willpower to make the next right choice. If we were to chart the good and bad decisions we've made over our lifetime, we'd see a clear connection between the type of decision and the condition of our willpower muscle.

The acronym HALT is a good reminder of situations to watch out for. If you are...

Hungry

Angry

Lonely

Tired

You might need to step away and recharge.

For the unmarried couple, the escape hatch from premarital sex is not asking God for strength to resist temptation while lying in bed together. It's the wisdom to agree to boundaries to avoid tempting situations. For the alcoholic, the escape hatch isn't going to the bar and praying for strength to resist drinking. It's the wisdom to avoid the bar and go places without alcohol. With lust, the escape hatch isn't asking for the strength to resist sin while looking at things you shouldn't. It's fleeing from places, images, and music which test your willpower *in any way*. It's sin to see how close we can get to the fire without being burned because in our hearts, we're open to temptation.

If you find yourself looking too long on social media, or realize that social media leads to pornography, you may feel helpless and out of control. However, you do control whether you use it at all and in what context. We control when, how, and what protections we put in place. We aren't helpless victims. Unless and until we get desperate enough to *flee from sin*, nothing will change.

Why test your willpower tomorrow on a temptation you can eliminate today?

That's it—Jesus' model prayer. As you pray this daily, God will lead you to focus on different things. One day, a situation requiring forgiveness will flare up in your heart. Another, it will be discerning God's will in your job. The Holy Spirit will work through this framework. *Prayer is* the single most impactful thing we can ever do. When we pray, God rewires our minds and hearts. Through prayer, God renews our strength and the Holy Spirit empowers us to be Jesus' hands and feet.

PRACTICE: EAT THE WORD

The prophet Jeremiah said:

> *When your words came, I ate them; they were my joy and my heart's delight, for I bear your name, Lord God Almighty.*[172]

Reading Scripture, along with prayer, is a keystone practice which keeps your fire burning bright. God's Word contains more *power* than anything else in the world. His utterances are so powerful that he *spoke* and the universe came into being. He *spoke* and everything as far as the eye can see came into existence.

His Words are *alive* and *active*.[173]

In this sense, Scripture is an extension of himself. As the prophet Isaiah said:

> *[God's Word] won't return empty but will accomplish what God desires and achieve the purpose for which he sent it.*[174]

It's a powerful change agent! As we center our minds on Scripture, it becomes a red-hot ember in our inner being. Jeremiah wrote:

His word is in my heart like a fire, a fire shut up in my bones. I am weary of holding it in; indeed, I cannot.[175]

More than words can describe, the Word *works* in us. Through Scripture, the Holy Spirit creates a hunger and urgency to see his will done and the Kingdom established. David wrote, "Our soul longs for the living God." Jesus said, "Those who hunger and thirst for righteousness will be satisfied."[176] The more we read, the hungrier we are to read. As we speak God's words, it sparks a fire in others as well.

God told Jeremiah:

Say whatever I command and write all the words I've spoken to you.[177]

To Habakkuk:

Write down the revelation, make it plain on tablets.[178]

And to John:

Write what [you have] seen.[179]

God lets us find him (his words, revelations, and visions) through the ancient text, first recorded in Hebrew and Greek. Like an archaeologist discovering a buried city, as we study

Scripture, we unearth a profound and beautiful narrative. As the storyline emerges, we see God inviting us to play a role in this intricate drama of rescuing humanity from the enemy's grasp. Scripture reorients our perspective from the temporal (what we can see with our eyes) to the eternal (the significance of each day, interaction, and action).

It's more than a book. It's the breath—the living Spirit—of God. It's his essence in word form. The practice of reading Scripture is therefore powerful, life-changing, and dynamic. Reading will change your life.

Pointing to Jesus

The ancient collection of writings contains immeasurable depth, patterns, principles, and lessons. The Old *and* New Testaments are valuable. Both point to Jesus as the climax of human history. Jesus explained as much when breaking down Scripture to his apprentices on the road to Emmaus.

> *[He] started at the beginning, with the Books of Moses, and went on through all the Prophets, pointing out everything in the Scriptures that referred to him.*[180] *As he spoke, [their] hearts were on fire within them.*[181]

For some of us, the inner fire has dwindled. The passion for Jesus is dying. Listening to Jesus speak through God's Word allows the Holy Spirit to blow on the embers and rekindle the flame!

Continual Practice

Scripture reminds us God is personal and near, not impersonal and far. The stories show us he's an *initiator*. Adam and Eve? God sought them out. Abraham? God called him to leave home. Moses? God met him through a burning bush. Elisha? He was farming when God called. Peter? Fishing. In Acts, God encounters Peter on a roof, Paul on a donkey, and Philip on a desert road. What about you? As you read, God reminds you he initiates, and he can use *anyone* to accomplish his will *at any time*.

By remembering God's work in the *past*, we see him in the *present*. If we can understand his way of thinking, we see he isn't a formulaic bean-counter. He's a grand artist, painting with color, inside and outside the lines. Like any artist, his paintings have patterns. While he's unchanging, *how* he works looks different over time.

Seeking God Personally

We must do the work to receive the benefit. Shadow lifting is a pastime I invented where I watch everyone else at the gym work out. I like watching powerlifters bench press a massive amount of weight because I appreciate the work it's taken them to get there. But then I snap back to reality: I'm in the gym to work out, not sit and admire Gary bench press a small house. Yes, I can be inspired by other people's strength, but unless I pick up the weights, I'm not growing.

Spiritually, I've been guilty of shadow lifting as well. We live in the information age, with more content and resources than ever. There are more influencers, life hacks, Bible studies, podcasts, sermons, devotionals, and content than we could ever possibly consume. It's available, for free, with the swipe of a thumb. Herein lies the problem: we're shadow lifting at the spiritual gym.

We've confused *others'* work with *our own*. When someone else does the work to gain insight, they grow. When we listen to their revelation, we should appreciate what they've done and learn from it.

However, we must see secondary resources for what they are: *supplemental vitamins*.

They're great in addition to a regular diet of Scripture. They're not so great when used instead of a regular diet of Scripture. Many of us live on supplemental vitamins and are starving for real food. We're intimidated to pick up a Bible because we're not pastors with seminary degrees. So, we let others pre-chew Scripture and feed it to us. While it's more convenient, this stunts our growth.

Yes, spiritual influencers carry an air of authority and wisdom as they share stories, speak confidently, and wear nice clothes. I mean, heck, I want to be like the spiritual giants of our day. But I'm fooling myself if I think listening to *their* podcasts is *my* workout. Yes, their content helps, and it's wise to feed our souls good things. As Richard Foster writes:

> Many others have traveled on the same path and left markers.[182]

So while it's wise to be an avid learner, we need to make sure we keep first things first.

God made himself available to us *personally.* Jesus directs us to seek him *personally.* Reading Scripture *personally* builds our faith exponentially more than a secondary resource. It's because we're *doing the work* and *going to the source*—Jesus himself (the Word became flesh).[183] We don't have to live in extremes: *all Scripture and no outside content* is legalistic, while *no Scripture and all outside content* stunts our growth.

A steady diet of Scripture supplemented by outside content is the way to go.

God has always wanted us to seek him personally. Go back to when he freed Israel from Egypt. He revealed to Moses that Israel—now free—would eventually want a king like every other nation. While it wasn't God's design, he gave Moses directions to pass along to the future king.

Of all the directions God could give, what did he say? *The future king must personally copy the entire* law and *know it like the back of his hand.* Letter by letter, word by word, transcribing the entire law would take a massive amount of time. Then, once transcribed, he was to *keep it with him and read it daily.*[184]

One must ask: *Why?* Why have the leader of a nation spend countless hours doing seemingly mundane work? Couldn't the king delegate this task to free up time for more important duties and have people with more time and wisdom read and interpret the Word for him? No! God was making a point: Scripture is a practice which shouldn't be delegated. He knows personally consuming his Word sets the human heart on fire.

He knew the king needed a direct line to him. Yes, advisors, mystics, and Instagram influencers *could* do it for him. But it was his "weight to lift." Peter wrote:

> *We are a chosen people, a royal priesthood, a holy nation, and God's special possession.*[185]

Like the king, you are a priest, and God needs you to be *personally* on fire for him.

We can't lead others to be on fire if we're not. Or to put it another way: we can lead people only as far as we've gone.

If we're asking for influence but delegating or neglecting the practice of Scripture, God won't give it. Our intake of Scripture is directly tied to our strength—you cannot have one without the other.

We cannot be weak in the practice of Scripture and strong in the Spirit.

Jesus died in part so we wouldn't need to use an intermediary to seek God. Remember, Israel did ask, and God gave them a king (Saul, David, Solomon, and so forth). As Israel settled in the Promised Land and made Jerusalem its capital, it was Solomon who built a temple for God to dwell in (to host God's presence, which previously traveled with Israel in the tabernacle).

The temple architecture illustrated the barrier between a holy God and sinful believers. Only the High Priest could enter the "Holy of Holies" (the innermost room in the temple, where God dwelled). And this only happened once a year. A six-inch-thick veil separated the Holy of Holies from the rest of the temple. Symbolically, the High Priest represented everyone before God on Yom Kippur (the day of atonement), by entering the Holy of Holies on their behalf to make amends for their sins.

Today, we shouldn't act as if there's a six-inch-thick veil between us and God and ask "High Priests" to go into the Holy of Holies and pray for us. This is the mindset Jesus died to tear down. As he breathed his last, *God tore the veil in two*, symbolizing a new era. Now, we are the Temple hosting God's presence—there's no intermediary.[186]

Choose Your Hard

Making time to read Scripture is hard.

There's a certain resistance to this practice. Perhaps that's because the enemy knows how powerful it would be for us to sit down and really meditate on Scripture. To apprentice under Jesus and obey his commands, we can't read Scripture at a surface level. It takes commitment, time, and intentionality to study, think, and reflect. When we do, Jesus sets our internal lives on fire.

That being said, there are legitimate reasons we can't always sit down and read at length. Children, families, sickness, work, and spouses are all real responsibilities. It's hard to make time.

However, it's also hard to go through each day with a dry spirit because the intake of God's Word is lacking. It's hard to live without God's Word. It's hard to face situations, temptations, challenges, and people in need without a reservoir of Scripture to recall.

The question isn't: *Will making time to read Scripture be hard?* It will be (at first).

The better question is: *Which are you going to choose: the hard of making time or the hard of going without?*

The better choice is the hard of making time, because it has the best long-term results. Our lives go as far as our reading habits. They're interconnected, as Scripture constantly reorients us to God's Spirit and Kingdom.

Being too busy for God is foolish. I've acted this way plenty of times, but it's like driving and saying I'm too busy for a GPS. God's guidance saves time and energy in the long run. The Holy Spirit keeps us on the right path toward the correct destination. Without his guidance, we veer off course, take the wrong roads, handle situations poorly, and ultimately waste time.

Sure, we're moving—but not in the right direction. Like artillery, if our aim is off by even the slightest degree, we end up missing the mark by miles. *Activity* is not the same as *productivity*. Activity is doing a lot but accomplishing little. Productivity is doing what matters most. Jesus lived the most *productive* life in history without being too busy or hurried. Like an expert marathoner, he didn't waste motions or time on things which ultimately didn't matter. Scripture—like receiving coaching from our teacher Jesus—helps us do the same.

Journeys happen one step at a time. *When* we step, *then* God makes the next step clear. He reveals things one at a time. This teaches us to depend on his voice. After God freed Israel from Egypt, he had them follow a cloud by day and a pillar of fire by night.[187] He gave them over 40 separate instructions, step by step, location to location, from Egypt to the Promised Land. Could he have given them the entire route right after the Red Sea and been done with it? Certainly.

But if God laid out the rest of your life for you today, would you depend on him tomorrow? Probably not. And without depending on him, you wouldn't reach the destination. If we knew the exact route our lives would take and the precise result of each action, *we'd never grow.* Growth requires steps of faith, not complete assurance. We'd never experience hardship because we'd only take the easy road. It's better to walk the hard and narrow road—at least according to Jesus.[188] All this to say, Scripture helps us hear God's step-by-step guidance.

Getting Practical

Here are a few tips to develop a Rule of Life around the practice of Scripture. The big idea is that it requires intentionality and flexibility.

Where you read matters. Find a peaceful, distraction-free place and a consistent time.

When you're choosing time(s) to read, aim to give God your best and first, not worst and last. If you're a morning person like me, nighttime devotions are hard—we're not at our best. If you're a night owl, morning devotions will feel lifeless because you're not fully awake. In his book *At Your Best*, Carey Nieuwhof explains that we all have a window of time when we're naturally more alert, and this is an excellent space to do what matters most.[189]

Be flexible when life happens and you find yourself not reading at the planned place and time. Do what you can with what you have. Maybe you planned to read for an hour on the couch, but you only have 10 minutes on the bus. Use it! Perfectionism prevents progress. If you miss one day, don't miss two.

There are times when finding an uninterrupted hour is impossible, and you'll feel guilty trying to keep too rigid of a schedule. It's important to adjust expectations and give yourself grace. If you can pray a Psalm in the morning, great!

Any way you can open up the window of your soul to God's light is a win!

What you use to read matters. I'd highly recommend not reading the Bible on your phone during devotional time and leaving your phone in another room. Using a paper Bible removes potential distractions. To take it a step further, consider using a Bible without commentary *for devotions* (as opposed to using commentary *for study*). It's a small detail, but we can get so wrapped up in the *study of God* we miss the point: *spending time with* him. It's also helpful to have something to write on nearby, signaling to you—and God—you're ready to listen.

How you read—building a reading plan—should start with where you *are*, not where you *want to be*. My pastor—Mark—has read 10 chapters daily for the past decade. Doing this, he goes through the Bible in 250 days. After 10 years, he's read it 15 times front to back. This is amazing, and it's where he's at.

Our job isn't to copy Mark—it's to be inspired by him and make our own plan. Your job is to learn what fans your flame by understanding how God made you. For me, I pray a Psalm out loud and read a chapter from the Old Testament, something Jesus said, and something Paul, Peter, or John said. I know myself—I'm an overachiever with four young kids. It's a recipe for frustration in this season of life to try and tackle a more rigid reading plan.

For *my* flame, I need to sit and *be with* God more than I need to read 10 chapters a day. Some days, I'll read a single verse and sit with it. Others, I'll go for a walk, listen to nature, and then pray a Psalm. *Do what works for you, based on how God made you.* It works for me to be intentional and flexible. You can tell whether something works by taking a temperature check as you end your time doing it. Are you on fire internally or feeling like you've just read a cookbook? Are you more loving after or cranky because it took too much time? If you spend too many days feeling like you're leaving your time with God with no internal warmth, that's a sign to switch things up!

Finally, rituals are powerful. Before opening the Word, consider taking a moment to pray and open your heart to God. Most days, I hold the Bible close to my chest for a few seconds before opening it to read. This reminds me it's time to *be with*, not *plow through*.

PRACTICE: FASTING

Fasting is another cornerstone practice to build into any Rule of Life. Words can't fully capture why this is, but *it is*.

God transformed my life through a season of fasting.

After college, I thought about attending seminary to work as a pastor but chose law school instead. I worked as an attorney for several years before realizing law wasn't the right fit for how God made me.

However, I didn't see *how*—after a decade of practicing law—I could make a career change. A transition out of law would require a miracle—a Red Sea opening. Young children, bills, responsibilities, and my wife in pharmacy school did not comprise an ideal recipe for a career change. As icing on the cake, I was in line for a substantial raise at work. We were about to "make it" financially. During all this, it seemed the ship had sailed on my dream to work as a pastor.

However, I felt an urge—an inner prompting—to "knock on God's door." This led to a season of prayer and fasting. When God's getting ready to move you from one thing to another, the Holy Spirit often prompts an internal nudge to seek him on a deeper level. In this season as I prayed and fasted, the door to pastoring not only opened—it *blew* open!

I can't make up what happened over three months:

My pastor and close friend, Adam, was called to revive a church in another city and needed an immediate replacement at our church. Suddenly, there was a job.

Then, our financial situation changed, making it possible to take a substantial salary cut and still pay our bills.

Then, my childhood friend showed up after 10 years of no contact. We spent an evening discussing life, and he opened his heart to Jesus for the first time. We prayed, which we'd *never* done growing up, and as we prepared to part ways, he asked: "Have you thought about being a pastor? You'd be good at it." It hit me right in the heart.

Then, the next day at church, a mutual friend asked if I was applying for the pastoral position as if it were the most natural question in the world.

Then, the same day, my wife, Roseanne, went to coffee with some ladies from church. One of them, Libby, shared her story (not knowing what we were contemplating). She and her late-husband Jack experienced a call to transition from business to pastoring many years ago. As they prayed about it, God told them to focus on what he was saying and not on external factors (like money).

Then, in the middle of the night, Roseanne woke up and felt we needed to pray. As we prayed, we felt strongly to ask God to remove our excuses and fears.

Then we received a prophetic word saying we had "shepherds' hearts."

God was hammering a point into my stubborn mind: *I'll take care of "how" if your heart is for me.* I'm a slow learner, but this message was loud and clear. I felt unqualified, but applying was a question of *obedience*, not *competence*. I would have peace if I got the job and peace if I didn't. Every move I'd made up to this point was an attempt to go up and to the right—toward promotions, advancement, and prestige. But now, God was calling me to step in a direction of his choosing, into an unknown future.

To my surprise, Pastor Mark drove over to our house after my second interview. I thought it was to politely thank me for applying in person because we're friends. But, on our living room couch, with tears in his eyes, he handed me a job offer. As I reviewed it, the salary was *exactly* what we needed to pay our bills.

So, we stepped out. It's been one of the best decisions of my life, along with marrying Roseanne and having children. I could list out God's provision since then, but it would take another book. I say this not to highlight myself, but to showcase God's work in a season of fasting.

The Purpose of Fasting

The litmus test for a fast is whether it's centered on God. He told the prophet Zechariah:

> *Ask the people of the land and the priests, 'When you fasted and mourned... was it really for me that you fasted?'*[190]

Our ultimate satisfaction comes from walking in alignment with God's plan for our lives. If God's plans are our aim, prayer and fasting help us hear *his voice* to follow the right path.

We live in a fast-paced and convenience-driven world in which fasting is a lost art. Among many followers of Jesus, it carries a bad reputation. In the Middle Ages, people went overboard with the practice, fasting in combination with extreme self-mortification and flagellation. This is the over-zealous monk whipping himself in the rain to try and rid his body of sin—not too appealing.

As a result, we don't see fasting as a keystone practice alongside prayer and Scripture. But Moses, David, Elijah, Esther, Daniel, Anna, Paul, and Jesus all fasted. So did Martin Luther and John Calvin. They understood God's Spirit burns brightly in those who desperately pursue him.

What Is Fasting?

In the Old Testament, the main Hebrew word for fast is *tsom*, which means "to abstain from food." In the New Testament, the Greek word for fast is *nesteuo*, which means "to abstain from eating."[191] So, fasting is not eating food. In addition to individual fasts, we can practice fasting collectively. Jehoshaphat called for a national fast, the people of Nineveh fasted as they repented of their sins, and the exiles fasted during their return to Jerusalem while traveling on bandit-infested roads.[192] While it's a simple idea, it requires self-denial to go without food when we're used to eating whenever we want.

Fasting Was a Regular Practice for Early Followers of The Way

Long ago, fasting was an expected practice for any person of faith. Jews fasted twice a week, on Mondays and Thursdays. Early Christians, to differentiate themselves from Jews, fasted Wednesdays and Fridays. An ancient manual for Christian living, the *Didache*, provides:

> *Do not let your fasts fall on the same days as the hypocrites, for they fast on Mondays and Thursdays. Keep your fast on Wednesdays and Fridays.*[193]

Some questioned why Jesus' followers *didn't fast.* Followers of John the Baptist asked:

> *How come we and the Pharisees fast often, but your students don't?*[194]

Jesus responded:

> *How can the guests of the bridegroom mourn while he is with them? The time will come when the bridegroom will be taken from them; then they will fast.*[195]

Jesus also said: *When you fast…*[196] Some people argue he didn't *command* fasting. And they're right. He didn't technically command it, but he clearly assumed his followers would do it.

If we're to *ask, seek,* and *knock* (an ascending scale of urgency), fasting is the knocking. Although Jesus assumed we would fast, he didn't give specifics about length or frequency, leaving those details up to us.

Early followers of The Way fasted regularly.

While they were worshiping the Lord and fasting, the Holy Spirit said, 'Set apart for me Barnabas and Saul for the work to which I have called them.'[197]

Paul saw fasting as a mark of his ministry.[198]

The early Christians—under intense persecution—needed God to come through. They sought him with everything they had because everything they had was on the line.

The benefits of fasting are astounding. Our bodies constantly process food, so when we stop eating, we enter rest-and-repair mode. Fasting gives us laser-like focus. We become highly attuned to God's voice. As we fast, we remember who we are. Fasting as a discipline is a distinctly human practice—animals might fast for natural reasons, but only humans fast to grow spiritually. When we fast, we recall we are God's unique creation, purposed for more than mere survival. It reminds us we're spiritual beings in a temporary residence.

When fasting, it's helpful to *remove distractions* like technology, shopping, social media, and news and to *create space* for solitude, silence, and stillness. That's the beauty of it. The point isn't only *removal* (e.g., not eating). It's *connection with God* (by creating space to intentionally fill with God). When we stop eating, doomscrolling, and binging Netflix, we carve out space in our day and slow down our lives. We feel—through the void—how these activities are deeply ingrained patterns and, in many cases, addictions. If we don't pursue God while fasting, it's simply a miserable practice of starvation.

When fasting, we must guard our hearts against certain things. First, fasting doesn't indebt God to do what we want. He doesn't owe us a specific result because we fast. Second, fasting doesn't make us "holier than thou." We develop a sense of pride if we see ourselves as better than others because we fast. Pure fasting leads to humility as we remember our deep need for God's grace and pray for our brothers and sisters.

We guard our hearts from pride by fasting in secret. And God rewards those who seek him secretly. Jesus said:

> When you practice some appetite-denying discipline to better concentrate on God, don't make a production out of it...If you 'go into training' inwardly, act normal outwardly.[199]

He practiced what he preached. After John baptized him, Jesus retreated to the desert for 40 days. Luke wrote:

> **He was led by the Spirit** out into the wilderness for forty days. He ate nothing, and was hungry.[200]

Matthew adds:

> Jesus was led by the Spirit into the wilderness **to be tempted by the devil.** After fasting forty days and forty nights, he was hungry.[201]

Jesus' fast—initiated by the Spirit—strengthened him before his public ministry began. How did he do it? He went to a quiet place for 40 days. This experience marked a significant turning point in his life. He was in transit from one season to the next. He knew once he began public ministry there was no un-ringing the bell, and it was important to head into it with the blessing and filling of the Holy Spirit.

Fasting, modeled by Jesus, is a practice devoid of glamor and limelight. It's you and God in the desert. That's the beauty of it.

Practical Tips

First, consider the rhythm of fasting to build into your Rule of Life. It can be both a regular weekly practice and a result of the Spirit's leading on specific occasions. Also consider your situation and consult a medical professional if needed (pregnant, diabetic, etc.).

On a weekly basis, if you can fast, start small—one meal at a time. It will shock your system, and it takes time to build up to longer fasts. Also, it can be intimidating, so by breaking it down into small, manageable chunks, you'll build momentum and discover the practice's joys. A good place to start is skipping one meal a week. You can build up to two meals after a month, and so forth. The early Christians thought fasting two days a week was a good thing.

However, the idea is to provide helpful tips, not impose a specific regimen. Advice I found helpful was to choose an evening as the "starting line." After dinner, pray and let the fast begin. You may be tempted to "load up" on your last meal before a fast. This is not recommended. It's generally better to "wind down" (eating less leading up to a fast) to help your body prepare.

The following day, skip breakfast (meal number one). If you're going longer, also skip lunch. If you're fasting a full 24 hours, skip dinner. During the times you'd eat, pray instead. Go for a walk. Read a Psalm. Meditate.

For instance, pick a verse, like Psalm 103v1, and sit with it for the day:

> *Praise the Lord, my soul; all my inmost being, praise his holy name…*

Use hunger pangs as reminders to seek God. As the fast ends, mark it with prayer. Eat a light meal even though you'll be tempted to scarf down 5,000 calories.

God is waiting for a group of people to crank up the dial of urgency and fast like everything they have is on the line. Let's turn now to a new topic: tending the spiritual garden.

TENDING THE SPIRITUAL GARDEN

As you start the apprenticeship journey, God's Spirit begins transforming your inner being. Jesus explained:

...the Advocate, the Holy Spirit...will teach you all things and will remind you of everything I have said to you.²⁰²

This section focuses on the Spirit's promptings to *demolish*—or leave—our old ways.

As you're engaging with the practices, he'll gently bring to mind small and large things to address. The practices—prayer, Scripture, fasting, and community—are spaces you enter which heighten your ability to hear these inner promptings.

Let's say you're practicing listening prayer and feel convicted about a movie scene you watched last night. How can you know this inner thought is from the Spirit? Jesus taught the Spirit speaks for specific purposes: to *convict* (i.e., encouraging *demolition* of destructive patterns) and *empower* (i.e., helping us follow Jesus' way).²⁰³

Conviction happens when God makes us aware of sin in our life and is not the same as condemnation.²⁰⁴

The Spirit's conviction sounds like: *What you're doing is wrong.* The enemy's condemnation sounds like: *You're wrong. You're a failure. You'll never get it right.* The Holy Spirit addresses behavior and calls you up, while the enemy addresses identity and pushes you down.

The Spirit illuminates sin like a sunrise lights up a previously dark area. He reveals—over time—areas of inner unhealth we previously couldn't see. These are any behaviors or beliefs that don't bring us closer to Jesus. One way God strengthens the inner fire is exposing and burning away deeper layers of sin.

When we begin following Jesus, our souls are like darkened, unkempt jungles. They haven't ever experienced a gardener, trellis, or sunlight. As we allow God in, he reveals things—patterns, behaviors, and beliefs—which stunt our growth. The inner conviction of the Spirit identifies these weeds and boulders we've always lived with but never noticed and empowers us to remove them.

1: Gross Sins

Dr. Robert Mulholland, in his book *Invitation to a Journey*, expounds on this process of soul gardening. As you allow God in, he first reveals large weeds and rocks on the surface. These are "gross sins" (i.e., sins that are obvious to you and others).[205] They're *external* behaviors like murder, violence, and adultery. To put it another way, they're sins we do with our hands and feet out in the world.

As you engage reflectively in a practice, the Spirit's conviction may come to mind: *That was wrong. You shouldn't have done that.* The Holy Spirit convicts and empowers changed behavior over time. He gives you strength to pull each weed and lift each boulder one at a time. These are *big* changes. But they aren't the end of the journey.

2: Conscious Sins

As you let God deeper into your life, he illuminates previously invisible sin (to you at least). It's like clearing large surface weeds away only to find a deeper layer of smaller weeds that were always underneath but unseen. The second layer of ingrained sin in your soul is "conscious sin." These are sins we knowingly do which are socially acceptable but don't bring us closer to God.

They happen in the *mind* (materialism, coveting, watching things we shouldn't, etc.) and through the *mouth* (gossip, white lies, bragging, cussing, etc.). While nobody may bat an eye as we do them, as we become sensitive to the Spirit, we become troubled by behavior incongruent with being an apprentice of Jesus.

Upon reflection, the Spirit's prompting may sound like: *Should you have said that? Was that fully honest? Should you watch that? Why are you coveting that?* The conviction is that a particular behavior—while socially acceptable—isn't bringing you closer to God. These sins are like dripping water on a fire you're trying to start.

The big idea is that nothing we do is *neutral*. Everything we do does something to us. Every action either brings us closer to God or takes us further from him. Removing conscious sins takes *time, sensitivity,* and *reflection.*

3: Unconscious Sins

The third layer of the soul garden consists of "unconscious sins." These happen in many ways. It can be *inaction* (not doing what you should), *compulsion* (an underlying behavior or addiction that overpowers your will), or *motivation* (doing the right thing for the wrong reason). They're unconscious in that they happen as "knee-jerk reactions" (they're behaviors

so deeply ingrained in us we don't have to think to do them—
they're just how we respond).

Upon reflection, conviction from the Spirit may sound like:
*Why are you really doing this? Why did you react like that? Shouldn't
you step in and do something?* It's easier to be aware of the power
of unconscious sin in the past tense (i.e., reflecting after it
happens). You may not have a conscious thought pattern as you
do it—because it's so deeply embedded in your being that it's
an automatic response.

We've dealt with gross sin (doing the wrong thing) and
conscious sin (willful sin that's socially acceptable). Here,
we listen to the Spirit's gentle voice speak to the inaction,
compulsion, and motivations behind *everything* we do. As we
listen, God reveals inconsistencies—splinters—we've lived
with for quite some time. Here are a few examples to help
drive home the idea.

Lust

Like most men, Ben struggles with lust. As he practiced a Rule
of Life, one day in prayer, the Holy Spirit convicted him of his
pornography use and an emotional attachment with a coworker
he'd formed at work (gross sin). As a result of this conviction,
he stopped watching porn and cut off that relationship.

Then, months later, during a discussion with his community
group, as someone else shared about their own struggle
with lust, Ben realized he was still sinning in ways that
were socially acceptable but didn't bring him closer to Jesus

(conscious sin). He'd been watching movies and shows with explicit scenes that aroused him—pulling his heart away from his wife. He'd also been scrolling Instagram secretly hoping to run across sexual images, and he realized his issue with lust ran deeper than he thought. As God's Spirit confronted this behavior, Ben opened up with his group about his struggles and changed his behavior (not watching explicit shows and getting off social media). As time passed, the Holy Spirit slowly worked in Ben's heart to remove these longstanding weeds.

Then, in a season of fasting, God revealed to Ben that he'd been doing the right things (no more porn or explicit movies) but he was doing it to please his spouse, not God (the sin of motivation, at the unconscious level). God also revealed to Ben that he was sinning by compulsively and habitually sexualizing women—always sizing them up as a sexual object and not an image-bearer of God.

This is an example of the progression of God's work in one area of sin. You can be further along in one area than others. For instance, God can be working on the unconscious layers of lust in your heart, and then open your eyes to a previously invisible gross sin of anger.

One additional example: the practice of prayer. In the Sermon on the Mount, Jesus talked about the motivation behind prayer. He wants us to pray with purity.

All these people making a regular show out of their prayers, hoping for fifteen minutes of fame![206]

People—in this case the Pharisees and Sadducees—prayed loudly in public places to be seen as pious. Recently, a friend showed me a picture a prominent pastor posted of himself praying on Instagram. While I don't know his motivations, it appeared disingenuous, and this type of preening doesn't fool Jesus. He taught that prayer isn't about display, volume, complexity, or length. That's all a pretense—it's preening before people.

In Proverbs, we read:

> A person may think their own ways are right, but the Lord weighs the heart.[207]

We can deceive everyone including ourselves about why we do things, but God knows the real reason. He "knows our thoughts before we think them."[208]

Impure prayer is a waste of time. While pure prayer from the Spirit releases tremendous power, impure prayer does…*nothing.*[209] Jesus wants us to understand that the motivations behind our actions matter.

David knew this well. He wrote:

> You do not delight in sacrifice, or I would bring it; you do not take pleasure in burnt offerings. My sacrifice, O God, is a broken spirit; a broken and contrite heart you, God, will not despise.[210]

He was saying: *I know You don't want me to just go through the motions. You want my heart. You care about my motivations.*

In another instance, Jesus said when you give to the needy, don't let your left hand know what the right is doing.[211] As a rule of thumb, when you do something good and the motivations are pure, you just do it. You aren't self-congratulatory and don't need to post a selfie. True satisfaction comes when we're obedient to God and know he's pleased with what we've done. Doing good with selfish motives steals the joy from secret acts of kindness.

When we allow God into our motivations, it's with the understanding he will purify them so we can do good with joy. We find life as he identifies and removes selfish ambition, greed, and pride and replaces them with a pure heart set on serving him. We deeply enjoy doing the right things. Otherwise, we're stuck in legalism—doing the right things with twisted hearts.

Blessed are the pure in heart, for they will see God.[212]

When we identify a twisted motivation, how can we invite God to straighten it? David wrote:

Search me, God, and know my heart; test me and know my anxious thoughts. See if there is any offensive way in me, and lead me in the way everlasting.[213]

As we engage in the practices, we regularly invite God to *search* and *test* us (to show us what's really going on in our hearts). As he reveals the truth, we let him *lead us in the way everlasting* (to the place of pure motives).

4: Trust Structures

The fourth—and deepest—layer of sin is what Mulholland labels "trust structures." Calvinists call them idols, psychologists call them attachments, and Thomas Keating calls them emotional programs for happiness.[214] Whatever they're called, a trust structure is anything you think you need to live a good life that isn't named Jesus. It's the foundation you see as necessary to build your life upon. However, if you choose the wrong foundation, when storms come, everything falls apart. Trust structures are usually a career, salary, relationships, health, house, children, family, and/or standard of living. But again, they can be anything we think we need outside of Jesus.

To be clear, none of these are bad—they're just not *foundational* material. Wealth is great, but it's not meant to be the thing you build your life on. If you make it that, you constantly live in fear of losing it. Your heart becomes wrapped around the trust structure you choose. And building on anything other than Jesus wraps the heart around an unstable thing. *Anything* other than him can be shaken and taken away.

John Mark Comer observes:

> *The great paradox of Jesus' message is: As long as you need your life to go a certain way to be happy and at peace, you will never be happy and at peace. Instead, you will live with a nagging undercurrent of fear...*[215]

We aren't fully following him if there are areas we keep off-limits because they're "foundational." *I'll follow you, but don't*

*touch my job. I'll follow you, but you can't have my family. I'll follow
you, but don't ask me to change my standard of living.*

Jesus doesn't accept conditional apprentices. He let the rich
young ruler walk away. Jesus confronted his trust structure
(wealth) by asking him to sell all he had and follow. The man
wouldn't. Wealth was the foundation he thought he needed
to support his life. He'd wrapped his heart around it, and in a
very real way, it became his prison. He missed the forest for the
trees. He stared at the best possible version of life and wouldn't
let go of his wealth to grab it.

Consider Jesus' parable on treasure:

> *The kingdom of heaven is like treasure hidden in a field. When a
> man found it, he hid it again, and then in his joy went and sold
> all he had and bought that field.*[216]

Dallas Willard commented:

> *Imagine that you discovered gold or oil in a certain property
> and no one else knew about it. Can you see yourself being sad
> and feeling deprived for having to gather all your resources and
> "sacrifice" them in order to buy that property? Hardly!*[217]

When we understand the life Jesus offers, there is no sadness
in making him our *trust structure*. In so doing, we find we finally
stand on solid ground.

Okay, deep breath.

This is the inner working of God's Spirit, which happens over time as you practice a new Rule of Life. Maybe during a routine prayer on Thursday morning, God makes you aware of something you said or watched the night before that's a splinter in your conscience. Perhaps during a fast, you recognize you've been serving at church to be seen by others a certain way. Or, as you lead a small group, you realize you need to let go of hidden sin to authentically minister to others.

The Spirit will partner and work with you in this regard. The point is to slowly orient your entire life around what God is doing by allowing him into deeper levels of your heart. Anything else is just building on sand. Let's jump into the next section: renewing the mind.

PRACTICE: RENEWING THE MIND

Formation Is Inevitable

As we practice a Rule of Life, God's Spirit transforms us into people with fire in our bones. Much like the right arrangement of logs around a fire allows oxygen in, an intentional Rule of Life creates space for God's Spirit to breathe new life into us. As discussed, the Spirit deconstructs destructive patterns (through conviction) and helps us follow Jesus' way (through empowerment).

Paul wrote:

Do not conform to the pattern of this world, but be transformed by the renewing of your mind. Then you will be able to test and approve what God's will is—his good, pleasing and perfect will.[218]

To summarize, *formation* is inevitable. We're either being *conformed* to the pattern of this world or trans*formed* by God through the renewing of our mind.

The question is not whether we're being formed. It's who and what is forming us. A second question closely follows the first: who are we becoming as a result?

There's no "neutral" way of life wherein we're not impacted by who we follow, what we do, and the things we intake.

Everything we do does something to us—it forms us. Paul said he was in pain like childbirth until he saw Christ formed in his people.[219]

Formation isn't a new concept. Rather, it's a condition of being human. According to Willard, throughout the ages:

…this has been acknowledged by everyone who has thought deeply about our condition—from Moses, Solomon, Socrates, and Spinoza, to Marx, Nietzsche, Freud, Oprah, and current feminists and environmentalists.[220]

They all agree we have been *formed* and can be *transformed*.

While they differ on *how* it happens, *that* formation happens is fundamentally agreed.

"Transformed" in Greek (the language in which Paul wrote) is *metamorphoó*. This is the root word for "metamorphosis."[221] Think of a butterfly. It's transformed (metamorphoó) from dormant cocoon to flying insect while remaining the same being. Likewise, God transforms us from a dormant to active spirit as we open ourselves to him. We're the same person, but he completely reworks our thinking, allowing us to understand and do his will.

Transformation Requires New Patterns of Thinking

In the last 60 years, science has caught up to Paul's premise on change from 2,000 years ago: *transformation starts in the mind*. Thoughts are powerful, like tiny rudders steering an entire ship. What you think determines how you feel. For example, if you think about a frustrating situation, you'll likely feel frustrated. Then, how you feel guides what you do. If you win the lottery, you will probably jump up and down in joy. What we do repeatedly becomes a habit. Habits shape character. And character—who we are—determines our entire lives.

Reverse engineering this, to live a life that glorifies God, *we need transformed thinking* (which impacts what we feel and do, our habits, and ultimately our character). As we practice Jesus' way, using a Rule of Life, this transformation happens through the work of the Spirit and our effort. We don't see it, but internally, God is working.

Science shows the human mind is incredibly malleable. This is called "neuroplasticity" (the brain's ability to change and adapt). For centuries, the scientific consensus was that once we reached a certain age, we couldn't change. William James, the father of modern psychology, claimed that by 30, character was set like plaster.[222] He believed children could develop character, but adults couldn't. You can't teach an old dog new tricks, right?

Wrong.

Creating New Patterns of Thinking

Modern science has thoroughly debunked this. We now know people can change their character over time by creating new neural networks. Our minds build these networks (connections from one neuron to another) as we do things. Doing something for the first time is like traveling through a dense jungle. We work hard hacking a trail in our mind where none exists. It's slow going and requires substantial effort. However, as we do the same thing over and over, we get better at it. The path becomes well-worn. It gets slightly easier each time we do a thing to do it again. The dense jungle becomes a clear path.

For example, I developed a habit of eating fried chicken sandwiches on my way home from work. Don't judge. There's a Chick-fil-A I pass every day right by our house. The first time I stopped, I hesitated and paused at the menu to see what to order. Over time, as I've gone to the same restaurant, ordered the same thing, and enjoyed it, the process has become automated. Now, when I pass Chick-fil-A, I salivate like Pavlov's dog, yank the wheel, and get a fried chicken sandwich.

My mind created a highway—an automated process—to speed up my decision-making.

This is how our brains work: they create highways to speed things up. These shortcuts are efficient because they free the brain to do other things or just rest. According to researchers at Duke University, habits (i.e., highways) account for 40 percent of our daily behaviors.[223]

Pause and Breathe—A Quick Recap

To recap what we've covered so far: we are being formed (first by the world, then transformed by God). Transformation happens through the renewing of our mind. We have a part to play in this by exerting effort to build new, God-honoring habits. The Holy Spirit empowers us as we work on creating new thought processes.

Knowing Isn't Enough—We Must Take a Training Approach

Nothing we do is neutral—life is a training ground, whether we know it or not. This is a simple enough concept to grasp, but it's not enough to *know* we're always being formed.

If knowledge was all we needed, we'd all be uber healthy, because we *know* the kind of food we should eat—salad, nuts, berries, and vegetables. The truth is we don't do things because we're *rational*. We do them because we're *habitual*. We don't rise to our most aspirational goals (running a marathon); we fall to our lowest habits (fried chicken sandwiches).

The training approach to becoming like Jesus is to stop approaching Christlikeness as an aspirational goal. Instead, we start auditing and changing our daily habits and rhythms in partnership with the Holy Spirit to reorient how we see life. By doing this, we become poised to do what Jesus would do if he were us.

Habit Audit—Most of Our Habits Are Unintentional

God transforms the mind through opening it to his Spirit repeatedly via an intentional Rule of Life. If you're anything like me, you have some good—and many not-so-good—habits. And these habits contribute to forming, or deforming, your inner life.

How can you know the habits you have? Audit your day. What do you consistently do, morning to evening? What triggers you to take each action? When do you do them? And what kind of person is this behavior turning you into? Remember, no activity is neutral.

This may be news, but most of our habits are unintentional. What we eat, how we dress, how we discipline our children, what we do in the evening—we likely never sat down and "chose" these habits as much as we just started doing them because we saw someone else doing it.

The point: habits—unintentional rhythms we pick up from the "pattern of this world"—form our character, which dictates how our lives go.

Nobody wakes up and thinks: "I want alcohol to make me so out of control that I ruin my marriage and break our family apart."

No—it's an unintentional progression from thoughts (I can't cope) to feelings (I feel stressed) to actions (I drink) to habits (I drink daily) to character (I am unreliable and lack self-control).

When we start following Jesus' Way, God doesn't rewire our minds in a moment. With the Holy Spirit's help, we're tasked with tackling bad habits head-on and building God-honoring habits over the rest of our lifetime.

It's important to recognize we have different starting points. We enter apprenticeship to Jesus with different beliefs, thought patterns, and values. We've been formed by the world, which is bent on molding us into consumers, users, and addicts. If you were the enemy, wouldn't it make sense to try and conform people into fearful and insecure versions of themselves—the type who compulsively watch but never act and buy but never give? God wants to free us from the world's mold.

Inner Transformation Is Freedom

Jesus models who God wants to transform us into: a person living in *complete freedom*. Paul wrote:

> It was for freedom Jesus set us free.[224]

This seems redundant: *Jesus set us free for…freedom?* But Paul was a master wordsmith. He used repetition to drive home a point: we're not living *fully* free. Jesus offers complete freedom (i.e., "life and life to the full"), not partial freedom ("life and life to the half"). Partial freedom happens when—like Judas—we encounter Jesus but remain stuck in familiar cycles and patterns. It's as if time stands still because we're doing the same things over and over.

Jesus didn't die to set us half-free. It's time to stop settling for anything less than complete freedom!

When I started following Jesus, lust was deeply ingrained in my heart. It started at 10 when I watched porn at a friend's house. This choice—although I didn't realize it—was like biting into a hook I couldn't escape from. In my teens, the addiction got stronger. I used lust as a crutch to lean on when I felt lonely. I wanted intimacy but settled for porn because I didn't feel worthy of anyone's real love. My feelings (loneliness) influenced my actions (lust). Over time, lust became a habitual escape. For 15 years, this addiction kept me from walking in my purpose, being vulnerable with others, and having intimacy with God. I was afraid if I let anyone in, they'd see what a mess I was. I felt God was constantly disappointed with me, so I stopped praying. My heart hurt, but eventually that stopped too.

Looking back, I can see the pattern of deformation clearly. The enemy uses the same bait over and over if it works. We become so defeated mentally we stop trying. We know we're stuck and feel powerless to change.

Are you stuck? Do you feel like you're living two lives, with a part of you no one can know? Is there an area of your life that's wounded? Do you turn to an activity or person to cope, instead of God? Please hear my heart: there is *zero* judgment. These behaviors are indicators the enemy has a stronghold in your mind, and you're settling for less than full freedom. Further, they're forming you into the kind of person you don't want to become.

We *know* the pattern but *feel* helpless to change. Get angry—the enemy is trying to destroy you. He's trying to wreck you, your marriage, your kids, your family—he wants you either dead or ineffective. It's time to fight back! Jesus didn't shed his blood so we could live in unforgiveness, sin, shame, and lukewarmness. That's the enemy's design, not God's.

By God's grace, *there is freedom.* I now walk in freedom—after 15 years—from my addiction. What I couldn't see at the time is that my freedom is bigger than I am. God frees us from addiction to help others do the same. Breaking addiction is bigger than you—God wants to free you from it so you can show others the hope Jesus offers.

Addiction destroys your life and robs those around you of what God wants to do through you. It's like throwing water on your inner fire while blowing on it. *We rob loved ones, spouses, kids, family, friends, coworkers, and neighbors of our gift when we don't live in freedom.* Yes, addiction sucks for the addict, but it's horrible for everyone else around as well. If you're feeling stuck, when—not *if*—you overcome, your story will unlock possibility in the minds of those struggling with the same things.

For me, getting serious about my addiction meant putting in the work and opening myself to the Holy Spirit's power to change. I entered counseling to unpack my mindset, triggers, and deep heart issues. I remain in counseling as part of my Rule of Life. I've sought mentorship, established a prayer group I regularly update (who've all committed to praying for our family), and regulated my electronics use. I don't do this because I'm strong. I do it because I'm weak. Five minutes of stupidity can erase years of hard work.

I'm not on social media, and I don't go on electronics late at night. I have a long list of boundaries that aren't necessary for everyone, but I know what keeps me safe on my worst day. We usually know what we need to do but aren't willing to do it.

If you're stuck in porn, you want intimacy. Porn *can't* provide intimacy. Again: porn *can't* provide it, like Cheetos *can't* provide nutrition. It can't give what it doesn't have. Often, we go to the wrong thing (porn) for the right reason (intimacy). The answer is simple: go to God. But again, we're habitual, not rational.

Stopping bad habits isn't enough to transform our minds. As discussed, we must fill the void with positive behaviors (i.e., a Rule of Life). Jesus said when an evil spirit leaves a person, it's like the person is an empty house. If it remains vacant, the evil spirit—like a squatter—returns, but with friends.[225]

We can't erase old patterns or force ourselves to forget mental images we've downloaded. We can build new patterns and strengthen existing habits that honor God. The Spirit renews our minds as we *remove* negatives and *replace* them with positives.

That's why spiritual practices (positives) are vital. We allow God to build protections in our lives, like bumpers at the bowling lane. We can't get too far "off track" with built-in practices to reconnect us to God. As we connect with God, he changes our thoughts, feelings, actions, habits, character, and destiny.

The Practice of Scripture Memorization

I haven't quoted Dallas Willard in a few pages, so here's one on memorization:

> *Bible memorization is absolutely fundamental to spiritual formation. If I had to choose between all the disciplines of the spiritual life, I would choose Bible memorization, because it is a fundamental way of filling our mind with what it needs. This book of the law shall not depart out of your mouth. That's where you need it! How does it get in your mouth? Memorization.*[226]

Jesus is a prime example of a mind formed around God. He "grew in knowledge and stature" according to Luke, implying he learned things (including Scripture) like everyone else.[227] Like other Hebrew boys, he likely trained his mind through memorization. When tested in the desert, he responded with memorized Scripture from Deuteronomy.

This wasn't a magic trick—he took years to memorize it because it was important. Throughout his ministry, he continually pulled from a vast mental library of Scripture to combat the enemy, counsel his apprentices, and communicate with unbelievers. To be like Jesus is to train our minds and fill them with truth. Great portions of Scripture to begin memorizing include the Lord's Prayer, Psalm 23, the Sermon on the Mount, and the Ten Commandments.

The Practice of Combating Anxiety

Can we train our minds to respond to anxiety like Jesus would? Absolutely!

Perhaps, like me, you follow Jesus *and* experience anxiety from time to time. While we don't always control when anxiety comes, we do control how we respond. Like David, we want God to test us and know our anxious thoughts.[228] In other words, this practice aims at letting God into the depths of our being because his presence brings light to dark places.

Paul teaches us *how* to train to replace anxiety with peace. His advice:

> *Don't be anxious about anything.*[229]

Wait, don't be anxious? It's not like we can turn it off. But he continues:

> *Instead, in every situation, pray—tell God what you need and thank him for what he's given.*[230]

This practice pivots on the word *instead.* When you have an anxious thought, *instead* of letting it run wild, pray. We translate anxious thoughts into prayer by *telling God what we need and thanking him for what he's given.*

We often feel anxious thinking about the future. We imagine worst-case scenarios and outcomes out of our control as if God won't be *there* as much as he is *here*. Prayer, then, is an antidote to our worries about the future. By praying, God reminds us he is with us now and will be with us then, too.

When facing anxiety, prayer is like Google Translate. First input the anxious thought: *What am I going to do? How am I going to pay my bills? How will I deal with this? I don't know if I can do it.* Anxious thoughts center on *our* ability. Step one is to become aware of these anxious thoughts creeping in and to slow down and breathe.

We activate our faith by translating the anxious thought into a statement of need. *God, I'm feeling anxious about our finances. We don't have enough to pay rent this month. I need you to provide. I need you to give me wisdom. I need you to calm my mind and body. Please help me to breathe. I need your help, Father.* Or, *God, I'm feeling anxious about this meeting. I need your guidance and wisdom. I need your protection. I need you to give me the words to say.* As we translate worries into needs, things shift in our spirit. By lifting our eyes from the problem to God, we remember our dependence on him and *his* ability.

In the same prayer, after telling God what we need, thank him for what he's given. *God, I do have needs. And I want to stop and remember you've always provided. You've always given me enough in the past—you've taken good care of me. No matter how this turns out, I'm thankful you are with me, I know you are for me, you love me, and I put my trust in you.* Thanking him activates our faith again, as we recall his faithfulness in the past. He was a provider *then*, and he's the same *now*.

As we engage in this practice, God transforms us from helpless victims into warriors smacking the enemy around in the name of Jesus! The enemy would love if we lived perpetually on our heels, playing defense, spiraling, hoping only to make it through another day. Paul urges us to play offense and take the fight to the enemy:

> *Take every thought captive, making it obedient to Jesus.*[231]

The mind is a battlefield, every thought a fighter (either for or against God).

The objective is clear: *take every thought captive*. The thoughts about our ability? That we're not enough? That we should harm ourselves? They are dangerous enemy combatants that need conquering. *I'm not good enough needs to become: God, I need you to remind me who you say I am. You say I'm fearfully and wonderfully made. You say I'm your child. You say I'm more than a conqueror.* For far too long the enemy has inserted lies, anxiety, and fear in our minds and we've tolerated living with these toxic co-tenants. God's work through this practice allows us to take back ground from the enemy until we can confidently say we are trained to take every thought captive and make it obedient to Jesus.

We don't always control what we think, but we do control how we respond. Every. Single. Time. *We are in control.* There's no gun to our head forcing us to respond in a specific way. There is always a choice after every thought. Like David, we want to choose to bring ourselves, and our thoughts, before God and to allow him to search them out constantly. Let's commit to telling him what we need and thanking him for what he's given. As we do, he renews our thinking.

Paul concludes:

> Tell him every detail of your life, then God's wonderful peace that transcends human understanding will guard your heart and mind through Jesus Christ.[232]

First prayer, *then* peace. Prayers don't need to be polished and wordy—they need to be honest, in the moment, and frequent. Fervent prayer produces lasting peace—a constant awareness that in every situation, God is near and in control. It allows us to release the illusion of control and return to childlike trust.

Jesus experienced everything you're going through (including the temptation to spiral when feeling nervous). Scripture doesn't explicitly say he felt anxiety, but the author of Hebrews wrote:

> We do not have a high priest who is unable to empathize with our weaknesses, but we have one who has been tempted in every way, just as we are—yet he did not sin.[233]

It's reasonable to imagine he felt anxiety in the Garden of Gethsemane. He sweated drops of blood and prayed face down on the ground, desperately seeking God. He brought everything before God and submitted it to him. And he left the Garden with peace that surpasses all understanding. Also,

Jesus was without sin. Therefore, anxiety isn't a sin. It's just a feeling. It's what we do with it that matters.

As God transforms our minds, he guides us to think, act, and become more like Jesus. Old patterns won't disappear, but over time, they grow dormant as we walk with the Spirit. Continuing in this vein, we talk next about the power of affirming our identity.

PRACTICE: IDENTITY AFFIRMATION

How We See Ourselves Drives Our Behavior

Recently, I coached my son's first-grade YMCA basketball team. While coaching, I met Katie. She was seven and a valuable member of our team. Every game, she wore bright pink despite our jerseys being neon green. Running shoes, nails, hair tie—she was consistently decked out in a combination of pink, unicorns, and sparkles. But don't let that fool you—she was also our enforcer. While I had to encourage most players to go after the ball, I had to beg Katie not to chase and tackle the opposing team.

One particular game, she was so aggressive I had to call a timeout and have her sit down. "Katie, I love the effort, but do you think next time you could not chase their starting center around the court until he cries?" As the game resumed, Katie sat scowling on the bench, arms crossed defiantly.

I asked questions to try and get at what was causing this aggressive behavior: "Why do you think you play so hard?"

She thought hard for a moment and tears started to well up in her little eyes. "I have to play hard to make my dad proud!"

It clicked—she was playing aggressively to impress her dad in the stands. I tried to undo the connection in her mind between playing aggressively and her father's approval. "Katie, don't you think your dad would be proud of you no matter how you play?"

Her response was matter of fact: "No—he told me I need to play hard to make him proud."

Ugh. Unfortunately, when I pulled her dad aside to talk, he didn't understand the dynamic he'd created. In her stage of development, with an identity centered around pleasing her parents, she desperately needed his love and approval. He'd made his approval *conditional* on her playing a certain way on the court.

Identity—how we see ourselves—is the *strongest* driver of behavior. We *do* what we see ourselves *as*. See yourself as a champion, and you'll act like a champion. Katie saw herself *as* a daughter needing to earn her father's love, which drove her aggressive play. The author of Proverbs wrote:

For as he thinks in his heart, so is he.[234]

Katie thought in her heart she needed to perform a certain way to be loved. And even as adults, we often use the same thinking. The premise is that how we think about ourselves determines our actions—so, how do you think about yourself?

We See Ourselves as Valuable Based on What We Do

As adults, we see our value as interconnected with what we do. While dogs sniff behinds and lions roar when they greet, adults exchange job titles. Have you ever thought about why this is? Why, after exchanging names, is the next question always: "So, what do you do for work?"

Why is a title so important? It's where we've placed our identity. Underneath "What do you do?" we're asking: "Who are you? Are you a person of value?" Has someone ever treated you differently after you told them what you do for work? Maybe it was for better or worse, but what happened is they categorized you. They marked you with approval or disapproval. They labeled you as either useful and interesting or useless and disinteresting.

When someone asks what I do, I used to say: "*I'm* a lawyer" or "*I'm* a pastor." In other words, I was responding: "I am what I do." Have you ever been without work and dreaded gatherings because you knew this question was coming? And why does job loss or demotion trigger an identity crisis? We identify ourselves by what we do, and in so doing, intertwine our value with our work. We're all Katie, working to earn the right to be valued by God and others.

Culturally, we value *doing* and *producing*. The biography *Steve Jobs* by Walter Isaacson illustrates this dynamic well. Jobs, an innovative genius, was notoriously abusive in the workplace. He categorized co-workers in one of two buckets: geniuses or "jerks" (although he used a different word than jerk).[235] Why? They didn't have inherent value to him. They were like widgets—either useful or not. I'm not taking shots. To be honest, it scares me how similarly I've behaved with people. Jobs represents an extreme version of a lie we all believe: life is work, and people are as valuable as what they do.

If We Aren't What We Do, Who Are We?

According to Jesus, this paradigm vastly misses the point of life: to love God with everything we have and love our neighbor as ourselves. Additionally, if we are what we do, is there value in not doing? Is there worth in resting, stillness, silence, solitude, laughter, fun, and people? If the only point of life is productivity, and we are what we do, the answer is no.

What strikes me about Jesus is how much he stopped—he was interruptible. He met people where they were. He rested, laughed, healed, napped, ate, and lived in a way that deeply resonates with many of us. When we identify ourselves by what we do, we strip away the very essence of our humanity. God didn't create us to be robots on an assembly line, getting gold stars when we meet the quota. Try answering the question, "What do you do?" in a way that separates your identity from work: "*I work as* a [job title]." It's a small rebellion, but it reminds you work isn't who you are—it's what you do.

If we aren't what we do, who are we? God, the creator of life, is the only one who has the right to define us. He has given us— followers of Jesus—a clear identity. The wonderful truth is God identifies us as his children, which is a status well beyond what we could ever deserve.

In Christ Jesus you are all children of God through faith . . .[236]

As a child of God, David writes:

I will offer You my grateful heart, for I am Your unique creation, filled with wonder and awe. You have approached even the smallest details with excellence; Your works are wonderful; I carry this knowledge deep within my soul.[237]

We are God's children through faith in Jesus. That is our identity today, tomorrow, and forever. We don't choose this identity; we discover it. Like a muddied diamond in the rough, we may need to wipe some dirt off—but we've always been God's beloved children.

Whether the speech you wrote changes the world or falls flat on its face—you are God's child. Whether you do well today or crash and burn—you are God's child. His love doesn't ever deviate from 100 percent. He doesn't love you 60 percent when you have a bad day and 110 percent when you do well. Win or lose, day or night, rain or shine, deep depression or exuberant joy—you are God's child, and he loves you exactly as you are in this moment, as you breathe this very breath.

This Identity Informs Your Actions

We know this from the story of Jesus' baptism. Jesus hadn't started his ministry, spoken publicly, performed miracles, cast out demons, confronted the religious elite, or toppled tables. Before it all, he was just Jesus of Nazareth, the stone mason.[238] He hadn't done anything to earn God's love. But, as he came out of the water, God said:

> *You are my Son, whom I love; with you I am well pleased.*[239]

God affirmed his identity. *You are my son—I love you and I'm so pleased with you.* Jesus's identity was clear and he acted accordingly.

Do you believe this is how God sees you?

Insert your name into that sentence and say it out loud— *[Name], You are my son or daughter, whom I love; I'm really pleased with you.* Does that concept strike a chord within you, or do you find yourself effortlessly shrugging it off?

God, as the prophet Zephaniah wrote:

> *... takes great delight in **you** and rejoices over **you** with singing.*[240]

In fact, "rejoices over you" can be translated as violently spinning around, overwhelmed with emotion (i.e., dancing). The picture Zephaniah paints of God isn't reserved and passive. He's a Father dancing with great delight and singing joyfully over you. When you were born, he did a wild happy dance and yelled: "THAT'S MY KID!" He's overwhelmed with you. He's spinning around, singing his favorite song, right now!

That's God.

And that's you. He loves you. He's pleased with you! Whether you're feeling down, unseen, unworthy, or unremarkable, remember the God of the universe *loves you.*

Jesus didn't earn God's love by "doing." He didn't gain identity through work. He knew he was God's beloved child, and his identity ("who") informed his actions ("do"). *Who* you are (God's beloved child) animates everything you *do.* Everything you *do* does not define *who* you are. Jesus acted out of God's love, not for it. When you know the *who,* you'll know what to *do.* Okay, enough rhyming.

The Practice of Self-Affirmation

If you don't already speak affirmations to yourself, consider getting an index card, writing down who you are to God in your own words, and repeating it out loud every morning. It could be something like this: *I am God's child. He loves me 100 percent. He's pleased with me. He's singing and dancing over me right now. I go into today with his pleasure.*

Even without a full understanding of what we're saying, verbal repetition impacts the inner mind. The central idea behind psycho-cybernetics is training an individual to repeat certain affirmations regularly ("I love myself"). By doing this, the patient trains the inner mind and eventually responds by modifying his or her behavior to conform to the affirmation. It takes time and training for God's affirmation of your identity to move from your head to your heart to your hands.

Greatness in Humility: The Childlike Way

> *I tell you as seriously as I know how that anyone who refuses to come to God as a little child will never be allowed into his Kingdom - Jesus, Mark 10v15 (TLB)*

As God transforms our minds, spirits, and souls, we discard unhealthy layers of identity. Jesus' followers changed how they viewed themselves slowly. At first, they saw their purpose as worldly greatness: power, prestige, and prominence. *Right after* Jesus told them to be humble, they argued about who was the greatest—facepalm. I often catch myself thinking along the same lines: *I'll be great when I achieve power, prestige, or prominence.*

When the disciples thought this way, Jesus *again* reminded them to be humble.

> *Truly I tell you, unless you change and become like little children, you will never enter the kingdom of heaven. Therefore, whoever takes the lowly position of this child is the greatest in the kingdom of heaven.*[241]

Children in Jesus' day were on the lowest rung in society. To be like a child wasn't climbing *up* the social ladder, but *down*. Greatness according to Jesus is going low, not high.

He said:

Unless you accept God's kingdom in the simplicity of a child, you'll never get in.[242]

Children are moldable and easily teachable. They simply accept things instead of dissecting them from every possible angle. When adults become childlike, a new world of possibility opens. Luke observed:

And the people of Berea were more open-minded than those in Thessalonica, and they listened eagerly to Paul's message. They searched the Scriptures day after day to see if Paul and Silas were teaching the truth.[243]

They were childlike.

What does this have to do with identity, let alone fanning the inner flame? Living based on identity requires an attitude of childlike wonder and curiosity. It's not a one-time revelation, but a reality we return to. We must detach from the adult way of analyzing and overthinking and press into childlike trust. Only the child will take the Father at his word. We must ruthlessly eliminate guile, masks, and fronts with God.

Brené Brown uses the phrase "radical candor" in her book *Dare to Lead* to promote being radically honest in the workplace.[244] She's not far off from describing being childlike in God's Kingdom. There's something pure about being radically honest like a child.

Children also rest well. Have you ever seen a stressed-out kid? The other day, we were 30 minutes late for school and our kids *could not have cared less*. David wrote:

> *I'm your resting child, and my soul is content in you. I will quietly trust, waiting upon the Lord now and forever.*[245]

My son never demands I show him our car's maintenance history before we drive to school. He doesn't need to know how the oven works before I bake a pizza. He rests despite not knowing everything because he trusts me. If we're God's children, and he's our Father, where's our rest? It's found in returning to a childlike place of trust, because we know we're God's children and he loves us.

Children know their parents aren't indifferent to their hurts, bruises, scrapes, and tears. As Jesus was traveling, two blind men cried out desperately. Their honest appeal for help *deeply moved* him.[246] He stopped and asked: "What do you want?" Think about this. They were clearly blind and Jesus heard them pleading. He could have put two and two together, but he didn't presume to know their needs, perform the miracle, and go on his way. He *asked* them what they wanted to dignify them and see what they'd ask for. They answered: "To see!" They were childlike, believing he could heal them. They weren't afraid to ask for *the big thing* because they knew who Jesus was. Then:

> *...he had compassion on them and touched their eyes. Immediately they received their sight and followed him.*

Over time, we lose our inner child—and fire. Life is complicated, painful, and full of responsibilities. As the weight of life *increases*, our willingness to pray honestly *decreases*. This shouldn't be. We don't stop needing God, but we do stop asking. Instead, we mask the pain with endless scrolling and another glass of wine.

We stop approaching him with the real story—the desperate cry, deep need, and audacious ask. We replace our unfiltered relationship with a cold formality. "I'm fine, God, everything's fine—are you good? Yep, great, okay." Or we don't ask *specifically* because then he can't let us down. What would it look like to be childlike again? Where is God calling you to trust, and where is he calling you to ask for the big thing, specifically?

INTERMISSION: WHAT WE'VE LEARNED SO FAR

But prove yourselves doers of the word [actively and continually obeying God's precepts], and not merely listeners… - James, James 1v22 (AMP)

Let's pause to breathe and recap where we are.

The last several chapters emphasized *how* to fan the inner flame. We've covered forming new practices and how they—in partnership with the Holy Spirit and our effort—lead to a renewed mind, behavior, and identity. This is the lifetime work of an apprentice. As we allow the transformation of the Holy Spirit to compound, God shifts our daily focus to Jesus, who becomes the center of everything we think and do.

The journey is beautiful.

Like a rising sun becoming increasingly visible over the horizon, God reveals more of himself as we slowly but surely follow his path.

> God's sunrise will break in upon us, shining on those in the darkness, those sitting in the shadow of death, then showing us the way, one foot at a time, down the path of peace.[247]

Every step we take is with an awareness of God's presence. God reveals that life isn't a disconnected set of steps but a guided path toward himself. This path always existed but remained a mystery until he opened our eyes. So what do we do? Take one step at a time. This is the process of becoming more like Jesus ("sanctification").

How do we become like someone? Simple: copy them. Find out what they do and do that. Plagiarism is the highest form of flattery. To become more like Jesus, the Holy Spirit empowers us to emulate his lifestyle. We aren't reinventing the wheel; rather, we're returning to the simple roots of what it means to follow Jesus.

Every choice we make forms us—it casts a vote for who we are becoming. We have an internal war always happening between the Spirit and our old nature (the flesh). Picture two buckets balancing on opposite ends of a beam, one labeled "Spirit," the other, "old nature." Each action we take is a pebble placed in one of the buckets. When we choose actions the Spirit desires, we strengthen the Spirit in us—and become more inclined to make the next right decision. But when we act out of our old nature, it grows stronger too.

As we walk in connection with God, the Spirit produces "fruit" in our lives:

Love, joy, peace, patience, kindness, goodness, faithfulness, gentleness, and self-control.[248]

On the other hand, old-nature choices include:

Sexual immorality, lustful thoughts, pornography, chasing after things instead of God, manipulating others, hatred of those who get in your way, senseless arguments, resentment when others are favored, temper tantrums, angry quarrels, only thinking of yourself, being in love with your own opinions, being envious of the blessings of others, murder, uncontrolled addictions, wild parties, and all other similar behavior.[249]

In life, we often fail to live like Jesus and feel hopeless after repeated failures. Jesus explained the concept of obedience to his apprentices like this:

If you love me, you will do what I command.[250]

When we are in love with him, we naturally do what he tells us to. Obedience is the natural response to love.

We often switch this around—like Katie—and try to obey our way back into God's love. When we fail, either by action or inaction, we try in vain to be better. And it may work temporarily. We feel inspired and motivated, but then fail again and become even more dejected. Jesus' way takes us to the root: relationship. It's there we find the real issue: our disobedience is an attempt to fill a relational void only God can fill with something other than him.

When we fail, the answer isn't to try harder. We failed because we lacked strength, so it doesn't make sense to run the same play again. It's a sign of self-righteousness, as trying harder shows we think failure or success is tied to our ability. Instead, we try differently (recognizing our weaknesses) with the right perspective (depending on God and remembering his grace).

As we close the practices section, it's important to offer perspective and set expectations correctly. You may feel overwhelmed, dejected by failure, and ready to give up at points in the process. And if you're starting a journey, it's essential to have a plan (practices which form a Rule of Life) *and* perspective (wisdom for the overall trek). The focus of the next several sections is perspective and wisdom to help you remain centered as you journey.

TRUTH: TRANSFORMATION TAKES TIME

Becoming like Jesus is slow work. There isn't one instance in Scripture of God transforming a person's character overnight. Identity, yes. Character, no. That's not how it works. Often, we want God to change our character through a spiritual experience, but God's growth is slow as we practice what Eugene Peterson calls a long obedience in the same direction.

As Dallas Willard writes:

> *Spiritual formation in Christ is... not a mysterious, irrational, possibly hysterical process: something that strikes like lightning... Spiritual experiences (Paul on the Damascus road, and so on) do not constitute spiritual formation...*"

Rather, it is:

> *... something we are responsible for before God and can set about achieving in a sensible, systematic manner.*[251]

As we follow Jesus using a Rule of Life, God molds our character like ocean waves smooth a jagged rock. Becoming like Jesus feels glacially slow, especially for achievers wired to produce. We want to grow *now*, and despite intense effort, quickly find we can't short-circuit the process. The mature apprentice accepts this and doesn't rush.

There is no "I've arrived" when it comes to following Jesus.

There are always deeper ways to grow closer to God. Maturity isn't rushing to reach a state of perfection or reflecting on how great we've become. On the contrary, it's becoming increasingly aware of how messed up we are and learning to lean on God's amazing grace. As we journey with God, we develop an internal peace regarding where he has us in the process at any given moment.

Grow Like a Tree

Becoming like Jesus internally is similar to planting a tiny mustard seed in a garden. God will grow it into a mighty tree, but it's a process. The growth of trees is a helpful metaphor, which is why Jesus talked extensively about them in his teachings and parables. Apart from "God" and "humans," "trees" are the most frequently mentioned living thing in the Bible.[252]

> *The righteous will flourish like a palm tree, they will grow like a cedar of Lebanon; planted in the house of the Lord, they will flourish in the courts of our God.*[253]

If—as Jesus says—good trees produce good fruit, how does one become a "good tree"?[254] Well, *slowly*—the process can't be microwaved. Every single tree you see requires sunlight, water, nutritious soil, and *time* to be what it is. God says we grow like trees, but we don't want to grow like trees.

However, quick growth is often cancerous. It produces unsteadiness because we get "top heavy." When trees shoot up too quickly, they don't have time to develop a strong trunk or root system. Their "top" outweighs the bottom. The fall is simply an inevitable matter of time. If we achieve quick results, we will fall by receiving too much responsibility and influence before we've developed the root system to sustain them.

Falls hurt us and others. The very thing that is a blessing in God's timing—growth—becomes a curse in our own timing. There's no year-long apprenticeship to Jesus and no such thing as mastering the practice of continual awareness of God in a decade. Brother Lawrence reported it took him *over 30 years* of intentional practice in a monastery to feel decent at "abiding" with God. As followers of Jesus, we commit to slow growth, patience, and enjoying God's companionship along the way.

There are many "oak trees"—mature followers of Jesus—to look to as examples. You may even feel like an acorn next to them. However, we must look at oak trees with the correct perspective: they're still on a journey of following Jesus themselves, albeit further down the road. We should be able to take wisdom from oak trees while not idolizing them. Paul said as much when he wrote:

Don't follow me—follow me as I follow Christ.[255]

To turn oak trees into idols is to create an unhealthy cult of personality. We become disciples of Paul, Apollos, and Peter, not Jesus.

Everyone sins. The failures of Paul, Daniel, and Nehemiah weren't recorded in Scripture, but Romans 3v23 reveals *all* have sinned and fall short of the glory of God. We live in a culture where it's easy to turn *mentors* into *idols*. Then, when they "fall" (i.e., be human), we're crushed. We are to:

Grow up in every way into him who is the head, into Christ.[256]

Don't be discouraged if everyone comes across as perfectly developed in character and devoid of sin—they're not. Stay focused and remember *everyone* grows slowly.

Stages of Growth: Childhood, Youth, and Adulthood

Character growth takes time, and there are stages of development. Although Jesus didn't talk about them much, once—in his final recorded talk with Peter—he discussed two "chapters" of life. After the resurrection (and Peter's denial), Jesus met him on a beach. As the conversation ended, he talked to Peter about his youth. When Peter was young, Jesus explained, he went where he wanted. Jesus then cast vision for Peter's next season of life: a willingness to be led by God where he didn't want to go.[257]

God is equally available to us in each season, but how we interact with him changes based on our inner development. Saint Basil the Great developed a framework for the stages of character growth. His theory is we all go through a spiritual childhood, youth, and adulthood.[258]

We find an excellent example of these stages in Moses' life. We often highlight his achievements in the latter stages of life: returning to Egypt, the plagues, the Red Sea, the Ten

Commandments, etc. But he was *80* when all that started. His 120-year life consisted of 40 years in Egypt (childhood), 40 in the desert (youth), and 40 leading Israel (adulthood).

Childhood

When we begin following Christ, we are "born again." While we are decades old *physically*, we are newborns *spiritually*. Like a baby, we enter a steep growth curve as we relearn everything we thought we knew. St. Basil wrote:

> *As we have learned from Paul, the Corinthians were babes; therefore they still needed milk—that is, the introductory and simpler teaching of the gospel—because they could not yet master the solid food of doctrine.*[259]

In childhood, we're eager to learn. We position ourselves in places of receiving, learning, and growing in a healthy faith community with mentors. This is a beautiful season full of excitement. However, God doesn't intend for us to stay children forever.

As a child, Moses was eager. He battled impulsiveness and pride. Pharaoh's daughter raised him in a royal household and he grew up with a silver spoon. While we know little of his day-to-day life, at 40, one instance revealed his childish character. As a royal, he saw an Egyptian beating a fellow Israelite. While Egyptians raised him, he knew he was an Israelite. Watching the assault provoked something in him and he sprang into action. After killing the Egyptian, he buried the body. The whole encounter happened quickly, probably within a few minutes.

His life would never be the same.

Children's hearts burn brightly in many beautiful ways. They have an innate sense of justice. However, in pursuing a righteous cause, children often take matters into their own hands. While we are to stand up for the oppressed, we are also to leave vengeance to God (or Mom and Dad)—children don't get to play the punisher. Children have good instincts but battle the enemies of impulsivity, pride, and lack of experience.

As a result of the murder, the Egyptians chased Moses out of Egypt. If he didn't murder the Egyptian, God could have used him differently to enact the change his heart burned for. God used Nehemiah, Daniel, and Esther—working *within* foreign governments—to bring widespread change for his people. But, because of Moses' impulsivity, he lost his influence in a matter of moments. He went from one of the most powerful people in the world to nobody.

His platform outpaced his character.

Youth

Like Peter Pan, many stay children forever. God uses humbling and painful circumstances to help us grow from spiritual "babes" into "young adults." For the next 40 years, Moses lived in exile as a shepherd. It was a shocking turn of events. St. Basil describes spiritual adolescence:

> *That person is young in soul who is perfectly taught in all branches of the virtue, who is fervent in spirit [Acts 18v25], who*

is eager for the practices of piety, and who being in his prime is vigorous in every way for the performance of good works.[260]

There is a certain energy, vigor, and drive youth have. It's their strength. They can do what children can't do due to lack of skill and elders can't due to lack of energy. However, the "youth" season requires *humility*.

Put yourself in Moses' sandals—how would you feel being banished from Egypt to tend sheep?

Angry. *God, I was sticking up for your people. For you! And you do this to me? You have me watching sheep? Feeding sheep? Herding sheep? Stepping in sheep doo-doo? I'm a highly educated prince! I can do more than this!* Moses would have naturally felt prideful about his abilities and where God had him. I've had my days, after switching from attorney to pastor, of stepping in proverbial sheep dung. *God, I switched for you—and this is what you have me doing? Three years of law school and a law degree, and I'm moving tables? Cleaning up after middle schoolers? I can do more than this!*

Underneath anger is hurt and pride. Hurt because we feel God owes us and pride because we think we're above what God has us doing. God wants to use us, but to do so, he must break us of entitlement. He doesn't owe us anything, nor do we impress him with our resumé. Forty-year-old Moses—while full of vigor and drive—couldn't lead Israel because he wasn't yet humble.

Over 40 years in the desert, God refined him into a man of character, contemplation, and virtue. Silence and solitude marked his existence. The days were quiet as he sat for hours tending his flock. He never became perfect, but he sure became humble. It's later written:

Moses was a very humble man, more humble than anyone else on the face of the earth.[261]

Shepherding for 40 years will do that to you. God uses humbling seasons to smooth away hard edges, impulsivity, and pride.

Does God have you "caring for sheep" with no end in sight? Are you doing "insignificant" things the world doesn't see? Good! Be the best version of your role possible, knowing he's working!

Adulthood

At 80, Moses entered spiritual adulthood. There wasn't a big ceremony; God simply appeared in a burning bush and told him to return to Egypt. Moses no longer felt so self-assured that he was "ready." He'd become dependent on God. St. Basil wrote:

...that person is old and venerable in soul who has been perfected in prudence.[262]

In modern language: spiritual adults have a mature and intimate knowledge of God. They're time-tested, thoughtful, and surrendered. While they may not be driven like a young adult, life experience helps them see patterns and pick the best path forward. They govern themselves well, and God trusts them to care for others.[263] Saint Teresa of Avila said:

When one reaches the highest degree of human maturity, one has only one question left: How can I be helpful?[264]

Adults know they exist to serve others.

I love my five-year-old daughter, Evelyn, but I wouldn't hire her to babysit our one-year-old, Daniel. If I did, and if I left for a few hours, I'd return to Daniel in a sparkling pink dress covered in makeup. We—simple as we are—know we shouldn't hire children to babysit. In the same vein, God "hires" (i.e., calls) adults to take on positions of heightened responsibility. Although we know this in principle, we often ask for things we're not yet able to handle. *God, give me a platform. Give me a church. Give me a promotion. Give me a spouse. Give me children. I'm ready!* This isn't *bad*—God seems to love audaciousness. However, we have no idea what we're asking for, and we most certainly are never "ready" without a deep dependence on him.

Moses, now a spiritual adult, trusted God to use him to lead others (in this case, an entire nation). He was no longer the young, impulsive child prone to outbursts. He was self-controlled, aware of his limits, and obedient to God's call. He never graduated from learning, and he remained a lifelong student. He wasn't perfect—God continued to test him in different ways (his impulsivity coming out later in life). He was simply a man who God grew over time to lead a movement. So, character growth takes time, and there are "stages" of development. How does God develop us? *Tests.*

Testing

Like an archer loading his bow, God stretches the most those he plans to shoot the furthest. He sees the target and knows how far you must be pulled back (i.e., tested) to get there. However, testing isn't enough—it's how we respond.

God's first exam for Moses wasn't the Red Sea. Slowly, he gave Moses more opportunity. He refined his mind, spirit, and soul to prepare for bigger moments. Once at the Red Sea, there was no way out but through. God led Israel to a dead end—water on one side, murderous Egyptians on the other. Sometimes, God puts us in spaces and seasons of complete dependence to force our hand: either we trust him or we don't. There is no play or strategy when we're in an impossible situation other than complete dependence on God. Has God ever placed you in a circumstance like this?

Once Moses reached the Red Sea, the stakes were high. If he lacked faith that it would part, the Egyptians would enslave or murder them. If it didn't part, the Promised Land remained a dream. There was no going back. Moses was ready to die for what he believed. How often is our resolve that strong? In faith, Moses raised his staff, and God made a way.

There is always a staff to raise (i.e., a step of faith to take in each season of life). The test for children: will they commit to learning, growing, community, and mentorship? The test for youth: will they work hard, serve others, grow in humility, and wait (allowing time for God to do his work)? The test for adults: will they continually seek the call of God to raise their staff in faith and serve others using their accumulated wisdom?

Whatever season you're in, the question is always: *How is God testing me? And how can I respond in faith?*

Seasonal Assignments

Be prepared in and out of season - Paul, 2 Timothy 4v2 (NIV)

To recap as we continue in the "perspective/wisdom" conversation: character growth takes time, there are "stages" of life, and God uses tests as opportunities to grow. We're able to respond with faith in pivotal moments because we've trained the right way.

We become poised, in our inner being, to do what Jesus would do. We become people who would raise a staff if presented with a Red Sea and who would give their time if presented with an injured man on the side of the road.

Understanding the Season Helps Us Focus on the Right Assignments

It's important to know the season we're in so that we work on the right things.

Israel returned from exile to a broken-down capital city, Jerusalem. Everything was destroyed, including the houses, walls (the way to defend against enemies), and temple (the spiritual center of the city). They faced the massive task—and season—of rebuilding *everything*.

Often, we face similar seasons. *Everything* needs rebuilding—marriage, family, finances, relationships, *and* ourselves. It feels daunting to even start.

As Israel returned to Jerusalem, God gave the prophet Zechariah a vision. He showed him a lampstand (which, in those days, required oil) directly connected to an oil source (two olive trees). In doing so, God revealed the future: His people would be directly connected to the Holy Spirit, *the power source for their lives.* But the vision—a new reality—felt far away. It didn't change the season of rebuilding or the test of what to fix first.

They felt overwhelmed. God sent an angel to encourage them:

> *Do not despise these small beginnings, for the Lord rejoices to see the work begin.*[265]

Rebuilding is daunting, so God encourages us to start. Lay one brick. *Begin,* keeping the end in mind. *Work,* holding his promises close. *Go,* putting one foot in front of the other.

God rejoices to see you begin.

They first restored the altar (the place to offer sacrifices) and temple (the place of worship). This is a beautiful illustration of how to approach life: give the spiritual aspect of life priority over everything else. Not that other things aren't important—walls, houses, marriage, and finances certainly are—but when we put first things first, we get the secondary things as well. It's when we put secondary things first that it all crumbles and we get nothing. When facing a season where *everything* needs work, the priority is strengthening our relationship with God.

It's essential to understand the season and work on the *right* things. This wasn't time for Israel to update its foreign policy, write poems, or rest. It was time to rebuild, starting with the temple.

In each season there is a test, requiring focused work based on your stage of life.

Imagine you're in college and have a big final coming up. To prepare, you study hard, learning algebra through painstaking hours at your desk. This goes on every day for months. Finally, test day arrives. You excitedly hurry to your desk, and the teacher drops the thick test booklet in front of you. You grab your sharpened pencil, mutter a quick prayer, pick up the crisp white sheets of paper—as the words on the cover slowly make their way to your brain: "Bienvenido a tu final de Español."

You studied for the wrong final.

It doesn't matter how hard we work if we work on things out of order! How often do we miss the season of life we're in and work on tasks out of order?

How Can You Discern the Season of Life You're In?

A *season* is a period of time wherein you have specific responsibilities. We don't have the luxury of hindsight while we're in one, but we do know a season—by definition—has a beginning and end.[266]

As a child, you're in a season of responsibility for one person: yourself. Youth get more responsibility (finances, work, physical health, and so forth). Adults get even more—caring for a spouse, child, business, enterprise, extended family member, and more. The point is that as you grow, God gives you more to care for.

Understanding the season allows you to focus on the right assignments. For Israel, it was rebuilding the temple—nothing else mattered if they neglected doing that first.

Let's drive this home with an example: a season of life called "marriage, school, and young children." When I first wrote this, Rosie was finishing her doctorate program while pregnant with our third child. She had to do eight six-week rotations, often requiring extensive travel. This was a "season" because it had an end date. It was intense, and the assignment was clear: take good care of the kids while she finishes school.

There were many "houses" and "walls" that needed work (e.g., my job, writing this book, cleaning the house, keeping up with friends, and so on). However, if I labeled that season as "my time to focus on finishing this book," it would have been like studying for math when the test was in Spanish.

Without the empowerment and guidance of the Holy Spirit, I do everything out of order. I overclean and am mean to the kids. I overcommit at work and become too exhausted to cook dinner. I write and become mentally distant from God and people. There were many good things—speaking opportunities, church events, basketball games, etc.—I said "not now" to because they didn't fit the season.

I wish I could say I did it all perfectly and enjoyed the season because I was so holy and wise, but in hindsight it was extremely challenging. However, within the hardship, God grew me, and I was able to return to an anchoring thought when facing tough moments: *this season is about caring for the kids.*

Solomon wrote:

> *There is a season—an appointed time—for everything...* [267]

Each season has a purpose. Often we complain to God: *Why do you have me here?* That's okay! But perhaps we could add some additional reflections to our dialogue with God: *What season is this, really? How you want to make me more like Jesus through it? What are my "first things" right now? And how can I honor and appreciate this time, despite how hard it is?*

Nothing you're going through is insignificant to God. It's important to recognize, as the psalmist wrote:

> *Our times are in His hands.* [268]

Keeping the Why Before the What

As we talk about character development, it's important to remember God grows us to accomplish *his* goals, not *ours.*

Any pursuit—including apprenticeship to Jesus—can morph from an altar (dedicated to God) to an idol (a thing we worship). This happens when the things we do outpace the reason we do them. In other words, the "what" (engaging in a Rule of Life through a set of practices to become more like Jesus) can get ahead of the "why" (loving God and our neighbor).

Let me give you a *hypothetical* story to help explain this dynamic.

A young man is passionate about writing and decides to author a book. He wants to help people follow Jesus and know God's love. Every day before he places his fingers on the keyboard, he prays God will use him and the words he's writing. It starts as an altar. However, he unknowingly starts to wrap his little heart around the book in unhealthy ways. Prayers become demands, he has delusions of grandeur (of what the book can do for him, not others), and he develops unhealthy writing hours (waking up too early, for instance, and becoming a grouch in the afternoon). When his wife and kids "interrupt" his holy endeavor, he feels frustrated.

Again, purely hypothetical.

What would you say about this young man? He's missing the point of what he's doing. He's turned a good thing into a bad thing because he drifted from why he started: helping other people.

To put it simply: our spiritual formation is always for the sake of others. The litmus test, the way to tell if it's working, is by looking at the fruit. Are we loving, kind, and patient to those nearest to us? To our spouse, kids, parents, neighbors, and the cashier? If not, it doesn't matter if we check all the boxes, attend workshops and ministry conferences, and meticulously reflect on our Rule of Life.

To combat this drift of the soul, we must constantly realign ourselves to God's will. Jesus isn't a personal trainer, product, or step on the spiritual wellness ladder. The end goal of spiritual formation isn't a state of zen or even inner peace. Those are byproducts, but to pursue Jesus for our ends is wrong—he is the end to pursue. The "why" is love of God and neighbor. This motivates the "what" (practicing a Rule of Life to become people who would love like Jesus). It's essential to keep these in proper order.

God's tests reveal whether the "what" has outpaced the "why."

He gives tests on mountaintops (giving us victory to see what we'll do) and valleys (allowing us to suffer). Take Israel as an example. As the Red Sea closed, they exited slavery and entered a journey to the Promised Land—a mountaintop. However, they wouldn't set foot in the Promised Land because they feared the people living there. This disobedience led to a 40-year desert season—a valley.

During that time, Moses departed for 40 days to be with God and left Israel with his brother, Aaron. The people became restless because Moses didn't give them a return date, and Aaron let them build an idol. They combined all the gold— brought out of Egypt as a blessing from God—and made a golden calf. As they worshiped the idol, Moses returned down the mountain with the Ten Commandments. He was infuriated and threw the tablets down.

God was disappointed. He wouldn't break his promise (giving them the Promised Land). But—here's the test—instead of going *with* them, he said he'd send an angel in his place:

> Then the LORD said to Moses, "Leave this place, you and the people you brought up out of Egypt, and go up to the land I promised on oath to Abraham, Isaac and Jacob, saying, 'I will give it to your descendants.' **I will send an angel before you** and drive out the Canaanites, Amorites, Hittites, Perizzites, Hivites and Jebusites. Go up to the land flowing with milk and honey. **But I will not go with you**, because you are a stiff-necked people and I might destroy you on the way.[269]

God tested Israel to see if they'd let *what* they were doing (journeying to the Promised Land) overshadow *why* they were doing it (partnership with him). God offered "success" without him in it.

Moses responded:

> If your Presence does not go with us, do not send us up from here.

God replied:

> I will do the very thing you have asked, because I am pleased with you and I know you by name.[270]

We drift and at times turn altars (like growth...and books) into idols. We become overly scrupulous, self-reflective, and caught up in ourselves. Instead of practicing a Rule of Life to benefit others, we turn it into a way to look good or to gain prestige, success, and even wealth. Maybe the test comes when you cross a personal Red Sea—will you neglect God on the mountaintop? Maybe it comes in a valley when God calls out an idol you've created—will you return to him? We won't be perfect, but that's not the point. God never gives up on us. Jesus, the Good Shepherd, brings us back to the right path when we slow down, listen, and return to our walk *with* him.

TRUTH: PRACTICING A RULE OF LIFE ISN'T LEGALISM

"Grace is opposed to earning, not effort" - Dallas Willard

When apprenticing under Jesus, we want to avoid the extremes of legalism on one hand and vague spirituality on the other and find the sweet spot right in the middle: the unforced rhythm of grace.[271]

It's easy to develop a legalistic attitude when practicing a Rule of Life. In other words, as we exert effort toward the working out of our faith, we're susceptible to pride as we compare our effort to others' lack of effort.

We quietly label ourselves as "holier than thou" and more worthy of God's love. Legalistic people are hurtful and produce bad fruit: dead works, deep wounding, and burnout.

My friend Gavin said the practices are like juggling knives. If we catch the wrong end (i.e., do them with the wrong heart) we hurt ourselves. Certainly God is pleased with effort; however, it does *absolutely nothing* to make us "righteous"—that is all the work of Jesus on the cross.

Jesus and Paul repeatedly spoke against legalism (*works without faith*). They railed against practicing a Rule of Life that didn't lead to life. They saw the Pharisees as prime examples of this misguided approach because their actions originated from a legalistic understanding of how God would bring about revival to Israel.

There are 613 commands in the Old Testament, and God did punish Israel for being in continual violation of them (e.g., the exile and subsequent oppression by foreign governments). The Pharisees thought God would lift the current punishment—the Roman occupation—if the people of Israel finally got their act together.

To ensure people wouldn't even come close to sin, they made numerous additional rules around each command to act as protective fences. The thinking was if people followed these supplemental guidelines, they wouldn't even come close to violating the law. But by doing this, they turned something beautiful into an overly burdensome, joyless, and dead faith. They became so obsessed with works they missed God, and the eternal life Jesus offered, as a result.

For instance, one of the Ten Commandments is to rest by not working one day a week, the Sabbath.[272] The Pharisees added to this law 39 prohibited actions so no one would inadvertently "work." But the rules were exhausting, which defeated the purpose of Sabbath—rest! For instance, no one could swat a fly on the Sabbath because you'd be guilty of "hunting". You couldn't spit on the ground, which could be seen as "plowing". And you couldn't walk more than three-fifths of a mile from your house. That's how it went with every command.

Jesus condemned this works-based faith as devoid of love and the bigger picture—the Spirit of the Law. They were following the letter of the law so intensely they missed the point.

Faith lives on a pendulum, with extremes on either side.

On one end is legalism (fervently working to earn God's love and favor). This kind of faith is high on "doing for God" but low on "being with God." A lot gets done in God's name, but the way it's done isn't with him and doesn't honor him.

On the other end of the pendulum is spirituality. Jesus and James condemned faith without works (i.e., believing things in your head but not doing them).[273] Jesus assumed if you had genuine faith, you'd naturally respond by doing good things ("good trees produce good fruit"). James railed against the idea that there could be faith without fruit. He said that kind of faith is useless—even demons "believe in God."[274] This faith is high on "being with God" but low on "doing for God." A lot gets prayed and believed for, but not a lot is actually done.

On the pendulum between legalism and spirituality, where are we? Would Jesus encourage us to move away from legalism toward grace or away from spirituality toward practicing our faith?

It seems we in North America now suffer from vague spirituality. The 80s, 90s, and early 2000s were a time in which the majority culture was Christian. Legalism ran rampant during this era. Back then, the common problem was being too busy: running ragged attending church multiple times a week, serving in soup kitchens, going on mission trips, attending prayer meetings, and so on. All this activity caused many to neglect their inner health and end up in burnout.

As this happened, we swung from one extreme (legalism) to another (spirituality).

For those who follow Jesus now, the issue isn't working too hard. It's being so inwardly focused that we don't ever get out of our bubble to interact with our literal neighbors.

As Dallas Willard put it:

> Grace is opposed to earning (an attitude), not effort (an action).[275]

We label effort "legalism" and *may* do individual practices (prayer, Scripture, fasting), but many times we find the communal practices more challenging: weekly church, community groups, mission trips, soup kitchens, witnessing to non-believers, and so forth.

I'm not throwing stones—I feel this tension deeply as a pastor in the Portland area, a very anti-Christian pocket of America. It makes sense to start practicing our faith in a bubble when the larger culture is hostile to Christianity. The problem is, that's not how Jesus calls us to live.

Jesus attacked legalistic attitudes, not effort or the spiritual practices themselves. He never said practicing the Sabbath, prayer, fasting, and serving the poor were bad. He said not to do them the wrong way.

Spirituality isn't what Jesus contemplated when he invited us to forsake everything and follow him.

His call is transformative—it turns us into fishers of people, not fish depending on others to be fed every Sunday.[276] Jesus will build his church on *disciples* (fishers), not *consumers* (fish).[277] Consumers chase emotional highs at services, church hop for the best speaker, and equate hype with the presence of God.

This is an honest and necessary conversation. The proper response to receiving God's grace is living in the Spirit, walking with the Spirit, and giving every ounce of effort we have. It's committing to the church Jesus died to build. Paul wrote:

> *We beg you not to accept this marvelous gift of God's kindness and then ignore it.*[278]

Jesus calls us to be the salt of the earth. Salt, while ordinary, is a dynamic change agent. When utilized in different settings, it brings flavor, preservation, destruction, or fertilization. It has an impact wherever it goes. Jesus warned about losing saltiness—the ability to impact the world.[279] If we practice a vague, hype-chasing, individualized spirituality, that's exactly what we become: flavorless salt.

Faith produces action like one bike pedal moves the other— they work in tandem.

TRUTH: IMMEDIATE OBEDIENCE IS GOD'S LOVE LANGUAGE

As we walk with God, there are things he tells us to do, and *when* we obey matters as much as *whether* we obey. Rosie says that *obedience is God's love language*. Further, deferred obedience is disobedience. When God speaks, we're to respond *immediately*.

In Acts, we find Philip, a leader in the early church, ministering in Samaria. At the time, Samaria was experiencing considerable revival. God told Philip to leave and:

> Go south down the desert road that runs from Jerusalem to Gaza.[280]

This was no small ask. It would be like *finally* seeing revival in Portland, Oregon, where I pastor, only to receive a prompting to leave and walk down a dusty road to nowhere in particular! If I were Philip, I'd have questions. All the action was in Samaria—why leave? But God's promptings require obedience, not understanding.

> So he [Philip] started out...[281]

While Philip was walking on the road, the Holy Spirit told him to approach a particular chariot.[282] Notice God provided more guidance *after* Philip obeyed the first prompting. He went near the chariot and heard a man reading a prophecy about Jesus from the ancient scroll of Isaiah.[283]

Suddenly, it clicked. God put him on *this* road, at *this* time, to talk with *this* person. He asked the man if he understood what he was reading, and the man—a government official from Ethiopia—said, "How can I, unless someone instructs me?" Philip explained the good news about Jesus and baptized him on the spot. Church tradition says this Ethiopian official went on to share Jesus with his people in Ethiopia and was responsible for the spread of the gospel to the entire continent of Africa.

The timing required for this encounter is precise. Had Philip waited to start walking an extra five minutes, he would have missed the carriage entirely. Had he delayed 30 seconds, the Ethiopian wouldn't have been reading that particular verse. We begin to see God orchestrates appointments precisely.

The prompting to "go south" came to Philip at the exact time he needed to leave to encounter the Ethiopian. Not only that, because Philip was filled with the Spirit and sensitive to God's voice, he obeyed God's next command: go near the chariot. From two seemingly inconsequential commands (go south and go near), God used Philip to spread the good news to an entire continent.

But What If Philip Hadn't Heard a Specific Word?

Good for Philip, you may be thinking. He received a clear prompting from God (go south). That made obedience simple— he either would or wouldn't go south. Since you're reading this book, you likely also want to know if your actions are in line with God's will, and you wonder how you can discern his plans for you. This is a good place to talk about God's general and perfect will. You're in God's *general* will if you live by his principles and counsel.[284] If you're in his general will (walking with him regularly, in continual conversation), and respond to a specific prompting, to obey is to be in his *perfect* will (his exact plans for your life).

But what if you don't get a specific prompting? Say Philip never heard God say *go south* and was wondering about what next ministry step to take. Or say you're wondering who to marry, whether to take that job, move to that city, or [insert action]—and don't hear God provide a clear "yes" or "no"? Assuming you're in his general will and have made reasonable efforts to hear from him, if you still don't receive a specific prompting, then whatever you do within his general will— undertaken in faith—is his perfect will.

To put it another way, we believe in God, but God also believes in us. He lets us exercise agency.

It is very possible several different courses of action can be God's perfect will for your life—none may be better or more preferred by God in relation to the ultimate outcome he desires. At times, I tell my kids to go play outside. I don't have a preference whether they play tag or frisbee—either is fine with me. If we listen and walk with him regularly *and don't receive a specific prompting* like Philip, we can be at peace knowing we're in God's perfect will and can take initiative (with him). And if we take the wrong step in faith, he'll let us know and guide us to where we need to be.

TRUTH: FOCUS ON BEING FAITHFUL AND YOU WILL BE FRUITFUL

"His master replied, 'Well done, good and faithful servant! You have been faithful with a few things; I will put you in charge of many things" - Jesus, Matthew 25v23

What if we're faithful to cultivate our fire and obedient to share our gift but fall flat on our face? Did Philip think about the possibility of walking south forever? Did he fear rejection before sharing with the Ethiopian? What about Ananias, an early follower of Jesus, when God told him to go pray with Saul, a persecutor and murderer of Christians? Be honest—there are certain people you'd rather not receive a prompting to go pray with. Certainly the possibility of Saul imprisoning him or orchestrating his murder crossed Ananias' mind. God asks us to do risky things with failure as a possibility. These are opportunities for *faithfulness*. And Jesus promises *faithfulness* leads to *fruitfulness*.

The fear of failure often keeps us from starting. Risk is daunting. We ask God: "Where will this road lead?" and want an answer before we start. What we're really saying is: "I don't know how this will turn out, and I'm uncomfortable with that, so I won't go." Again, if obedience comes with conditions, it's disobedience. Faith is measured by what we're willing to risk for God. Although we want to understand how everything will play out and desire to control the outcome before we go, this prevents us from moving forward—because we can't know the future.

Using What You Have—Jesus' Parable on Talents

Jesus explained the concept of *faithfulness* and *fruitfulness* through a story.[285] Before leaving on a journey, a property owner gave three servants the task of managing his money, giving different amounts to each. To the first, he gave five talents (a massive amount of gold); to the second, two; and to the third, one. He gave money in proportion to each servant's ability, so those with more ability got more to manage.

After the owner left, the servant with five talents invested them and produced five more. The one with two talents did the same.

The servant with one, however, hid it in the ground. When the owner returned, the servants with ten and four talents explained what happened, and the owner said the same thing to each:

*Well done, good and **faithful** servant. You have been **faithful** over a little; I will set you over much.*[286]

The first two servants were ready to respond when opportunity presented itself. They were people poised to responsibly manage whatever they received to the best of their ability.

When the third servant buried his talent, he refused to use what he had. He was not the kind of person who was ready to respond with his best effort. Not only did he bury his head in the sand, he shifted blame to fault the owner:

'Master, I knew you to be a hard man, reaping where you did not sow, and gathering where you scattered no seed, so I was afraid, and I went and hid your talent in the ground.[287]

He saw the owner as hard-driving, insensitive, and unfair. When we have the wrong mindset about God, we see situations he puts us in as possibilities to let him down, not opportunities to lift him up. In turn, we do nothing; and by not even trying, we fail.

Failure is not trying. *Faithfulness* is trying our best with the risk of failure. Catch the difference?

Sometimes, we're so afraid of losing we don't even try—and by not trying, we lose. And with this mindset, we're prone to resent God for our inaction.

God doesn't make us the same. Each person in the story had the potential to be *faithful* and *fruitful*. God only expects from us what we can do. He knows our unique potential, gifts, and talents. You don't have to reach my finish line, and I don't have to reach yours.

God expects you to produce the talents he's hidden in you. It's fair to expect a blueberry bush to produce blueberries and an orange tree to produce oranges. It's only when the blueberry bush thinks it's unfair that it has to make blueberries—or lives in comparison to the orange tree—that there's a problem!

How do we get so mixed up? By telling ourselves powerful stories—about ourselves. There have been days when I've bought into the lie that I have *nothing* to contribute to the world. Doom scrolling on social media and seeing everyone saying insightful things made me feel in comparison I had zero talents and nothing to add. The comparison-minded person watches five-talent people produce five more talents and feels like giving up. But isn't that the problem? We're looking around instead of putting our blinders on and running our race.

Here's the kicker: *thinking* we have nothing to give causes us to give nothing.

We speak a self-fulfilling prophecy over our lives. Then we blame God. *You didn't make me an incredible speaker like so and so!* What we're really saying is: *You didn't give me five talents!* God responds: *But what did I give you? And are you using it to the best of your ability?* Don't be a blueberry bush yelling at God for not making it an orange tree—God makes each of us with a specific purpose, to fill a specific need!

Be *faithful*, and you will be *fruitful*.[288]

Jesus didn't contemplate the possibility of an apprentice being unfruitful—that would be a foreign concept to him. In the Parable of the Sower, there are four categories of people. Only the last category—the good soil—represents the apprentice. Of the apprentice, Jesus promises:

> *This is the one who hears the word and understands it. He indeed bears fruit and yields, in one case a hundredfold, in another sixty, and in another thirty.*[289]

The question isn't *whether* you will be fruitful, but *how much* fruit God will produce through you.

Redefining Success as Obedience

It's in this sense we need to redefine "success" as faithfulness and stop looking at failure through a black and white lens.

A story from my childhood helps illuminate this idea. I grew up *loving* basketball. I slept with a ball, had posters of Michael Jordan on my wall, collected NBA cards, and practiced for hours on end. I once beat my grandmother 200 to nothing in a game of one-on-one in our driveway, showing absolutely no mercy at the humble age of 10. One day, I dreamed of playing professionally for the Portland Trail Blazers. I put everything I had into basketball, and got good results for a while. After a successful high school career, I played *briefly* in college.

To make the team, I was first to the gym and last one out. Every day during summer, the strength training coach and I worked on conditioning, dribbling weighted balls, and shooting from every spot on the court. I was *faithful* with all 5'11 and 155 pounds of my being.

That fall, the head coach called me into his office and told me to shut the door. He was a New Yorker and direct: "Son, you didn't make the team. I'm sorry."

In that moment, it felt like I'd been stabbed in the chest with a hot knife.

All the hard work, dreams, and plans for my future came crashing down in an instant. Things weren't panning out at all like I'd thought. Maybe you've experienced this pain too. You gave everything you had to something or someone, but things didn't work out like you thought.

At first, we see failure in black and white. Either something worked out or it didn't. But when we view things from God's perspective, we start to see fruit in the "failure." Now, I don't see dashed dreams when I look back at my basketball career. I see character development, growth, friendships, tears, heartache, laughter, and a love of working hard. I see it now how I never could have seen it then. God used basketball to shape me and teach me about life.

Faithfulness is accepting that the results are in God's hands and that the way he produces fruit (pruning those he loves) often looks different than what we envision. I'd be a different husband, father, and pastor if I cut corners in my "failed" basketball career. And if the only point of the things we do is reaching the goal we can see, we'll treat many experiences as massive failures. But to view life like that is to miss the point.

Philosopher Arthur Schopenhauer said:

> *Talent hits a target no one else can hit. Genius hits a target no one else can see.*[290]

Perhaps, then, God is the genius directing us to targets of his choosing, which we cannot clearly see.

Many times, when we faithfully use what we have, we see predictable "fruit." For instance, the servant with five talents invested them, and it was foreseeable they turned into ten. But results don't always have to be expected to be a win in God's Kingdom.

Again, if we define "success" only by what we can see and predict, our view is too narrow. We can't see the scope, ripple effects, and moving pieces of our actions. Job questioned *why*, despite being faithful, he lost everything. God replied with 77 questions to help him understand only he created, controls, and comprehends the universe.

Many step out in faith and "fail." The church plant doesn't work out. The business goes under. The relationship ends.

But God's purpose might have been different than yours. Maybe the church plant was designed to reach one specific family. Is it a small matter to bring one family into eternal life? Where the church planter sees failure, God sees generational impact. Perhaps God designed the business venture like my basketball experience, to teach you about life. You never know what one small act of faithfulness will do. The moral of the story is to trust God to produce the fruit he needs to accomplish his purposes.

He promises to use *everything for the good of those who love him and are called according to his purposes.*[291] "Everything" includes "failure." We usually ask: "Will I fail if I try?" Perhaps a better question is: "Is God calling me to it?" If so, he'll produce fruit through it. There's no risk of "failure" when you leave the fruit up to him.

When and Then

When we're faithful in the little things, God gives us more responsibility. Like a good manager, he sees trustworthy and dependable employees and gives them more to steward. We often want more responsibility *before* showing we're trustworthy, but that's not how life works.

When I get a raise, *then* I'll be generous. *When* I get a house, *then* I'll host. *When* the emergency comes, *then* I'll pray. *When* I get the promotion, *then* I'll bring my ideas to the table. *When* the lead pastor calls, *then* I'll serve. *When* [circumstance out of my control happens], *then* [I'll take action].

When and *then* thinking excuses us from taking action.

When we wait for things we don't control to change, we lose impact and influence. The better approach is to focus on doing our best with what we have. When we do that, our influence increases.[292]

Jesus commended the poor widow who dropped two pennies into the offering box because it was all she had. She didn't wait to get more to give more. Jesus observed:

Truly I say to you that this poor widow has put in more than all; for all these out of their abundance have put in offerings for God, but she out of her poverty put in all the livelihood that she had.[293]

God knows what you have to give and rejoices when you give it—even if it feels like two cents.

When we strip away the excuses and victim mentality and become proactive, our faith comes alive. We might not have all the ability, money, time, or energy, but God can multiply the little we do have! Human math is one plus one equals two. God is not bound by these rules. To him, five loaves plus two fish can equal thousands of meals.

Faithfulness is grown one day at a time and requires practice. Paul said:

*Whatever you have learned, received, heard from me, or seen in me, **put it into practice.***[294]

We can study the idea of faithfulness all day, but we don't grow until we start doing things.

The time to "get ready" to manage five talents isn't when you're handed five talents. Imagine if Moses, at the Red Sea, hadn't put in the daily work to strengthen his inner fire. I can see him, sweaty palms and nervous speech: "Sorry, God, can we *maybe* do this later?" Thankfully, God built Moses' faith over time, and Moses was obedient. God moves mountains as we play our tiny role—raising a staff, fighting temptation, or leading a family. He will constantly strengthen us in union with Christ.[295]

David Was Ready

David was a scrawny teen, the youngest of eight. Like Moses, he spent his formative years alone, caring for sheep in the countryside. This was his life, day after day, year after year. He learned a lot through shepherding. He focused on being the best shepherd he could be. He used his time well, practicing slinging rocks on those quiet days to be ready if a predator attacked. Sure enough, when lions or bears ambushed his flock, he killed them. During down time, he also practiced on his harp and wrote poetry.

David had no idea God was preparing him to fight Goliath, play music before King Saul, write songs that would make hearts soar 2,000 years later, and eventually be king. He didn't "work his way up"—God called him up because of his faithfulness. His story would be dramatically different if he didn't work while no one was watching. If he neglected practice (slinging, writing, and playing the harp), he wouldn't have had time to "get ready" for the pivotal moments of his life.

You could label him an overnight success, but that would sell the years of training short. That's usually how life works. God sees the nights, quiet seasons, and steadfastness when no one else does. He hears the prayers. Keep going! If God begins a good work in you, he will complete it.[296]

TRUTH: THERE IS PURPOSE IN WAITING

Don't be impatient. Wait for the Lord, and he will come and save you! - David, Psalm 27v14 (TLB)

There's a saying in the financial world: the best investor is a dead one. In other words, invest and let it sit—don't try to time the market to make a quick profit. Years ago, I got into trading penny stocks (cheap stocks with lots of potential upside...and downside). To answer your next question, yes, I lost most of my money. When the penny stock plummeted, I sold. Or, when it did nothing for months, I got bored, and sold. Then, it immediately shot up.

This happened several times before I learned a valuable lesson: when you want to change course—when things are boring or the stock is low—wait!

Often, it feels like nothing is happening even though we're faithful. In these times of waiting, we get antsy and feel we need to do something different. We "shake it up" because we aren't seeing immediate results. But that's exactly when to stay the course!

Daniel's story sticks out as an example of patience and waiting. During Israel's exile to Babylon, he committed to fast for 21 days to seek help from God. But 21 days passed and he didn't hear *anything*. He kept fasting. Finally, on day 24, God spoke:

> *Since the first day* that you set your mind to gain understanding and to humble yourself before your God, **your words were heard,** and I have come in response to them.[297]

God *hears* prayer immediately but doesn't always *respond* right away. He grows our faith in waiting and silence. Parents respond immediately to an infant's needs. But with a child, sometimes it's best for parents to delay rushing in to fix everything to let them figure it out. That's how they grow.

God's silence can be a testament to the maturity he sees in you, not a sign of indifference. Further, silence can be a sign to keep going and not give up! How tragic would it be to give up a day before breakthrough—it would be like Daniel quitting on day 23!

Waiting requires trust. Often, we stop knocking when we don't receive an immediate answer, or we go ahead on our own. Impulsivity and unwillingness to wait derive from *fear* and *pain*. We *fear* God won't come through, so we take matters into our own hands. Or, we're in such *pain* we feel we can't take it anymore and move on our own.

Billy Graham said it well:

Mountaintops are for views and inspiration, but fruit is grown in the valleys.[298]

God does his deepest work while we're waiting in the valleys of life. In the broken moments and seasons, when we continue to trust and wait on God, he produces special fruit. There is purpose in pain.

A truth of life: the length we wait is proportionate to the trust we have in who we're waiting for. Low trust equals a short wait. When my seven-year-old son Andrew asks me to wait, there are limits to this request. Once, during a game of hide and seek, he left me hiding—folded like a pretzel in a dark closet—for 15 minutes before I realized he'd moved on to another activity. But with God, if we really trust who he says he is, we'll wait however long it takes for the breakthrough.

Here's what I do know: we're exactly where we need to be at this given moment, place, and time. God uses us *as we are* for his purposes. We can wait on him because he is reliable and trustworthy. He's delivered on all his promises.[299] If God says he'll do it, he will do it! Let's turn to the fourth and final section: sharing your fire.

FOUR
SHARING YOUR FIRE

WHO WAS A NEIGHBOR?

We've covered how our inner fire can be *stolen, sparked,* and *strengthened.* We've talked about building a Rule of Life through practices that draw us closer to God, and the internal transformation God works in us. This inner formation to be like Jesus takes a lifetime. It also requires immediate obedience and faithfulness to our current season of life.

The result of God's inner working in us is *sharing our fire with others.*

When people asked Jesus what the greatest commandment was, he responded:

> *'Love the Lord your God with all your heart and with all your soul and with all your mind.' This is the first and greatest commandment. And the second is like it: 'Love your neighbor as yourself.'*[300]

Loving God and neighbor are intertwined—one cannot go without the other. To put it another way, we only have God when we share him.

As we engage in a Rule of Life, God reforms us into the type of people who share internal warmth with others. The practices forming a Rule of Life help the Holy Spirit strengthen our inner fire. But—and this is key—the point of having inner fire is sharing it.

With Jesus, we become able to open the doors of our heart to share all we are with everyone we encounter. We invite others in to be warmed by the love of Jesus in us. *This* is how we love our neighbor—by becoming people of love.

Love Thyself

At first, we may enthusiastically respond: "Yes! We *can* share our fire! We *can* treat everyone like we want to be treated. We *can* be loving and kind to our neighbors." But while we can in theory, we often find it challenging in practice.

I'm not writing from a place of sainthood—it's hard. I'm right there with you trying to figure it out. I struggle to live out what Jesus commanded every day. I'm still learning to act like Jesus would with the people I encounter in everyday life. The other night, my wife woke me up because she had a bad dream. Instead of consoling her, I scolded her for interrupting my sleep, said something mean, and lay back down. *That* was my knee-jerk reaction. Suffice to say, I am a work in progress.

The challenge here isn't understanding the *concept of* love; it's being ready to love from an overflow of the heart. Jesus didn't say, "Well *thought*, good and faithful servant." He said, "Well *done*." We do what we are. Jesus challenged the notion of labeling ourselves as apprentices without doing God's will:

> *Not everyone who says to me, 'Lord, Lord' will enter the kingdom of heaven, but only the one who does the will of my Father who is in heaven.*[301]

When initially thinking about interacting with my neighbors, there are many reasons I might have a negative knee-jerk reaction to interrupting my schedule and *actually* doing it. It's impractical. I don't have the time, energy, money, or patience. Also, neighbors—the people I share the earth with—are different than I am.

When I think about loving my neighbor as a task, I tell myself in 10 years, when I have time, margin, older children, and more money in the bank—then I'll do it. In the future, when I'm not just surviving and searching for sanity—*then* I'll do some good for others. But not here, now. How can we approach what feels intimidating, impractical, and scary? Let's do some unpacking.

First, we're to love others *as we love ourselves*. Translation: we need to *have* love to *give* it.

To put it another way, we give what we have. Jesus taught we give whatever's in us—good or bad. Good trees can't produce bad fruit, and bad trees can't produce good fruit. If we have God's love, we'll give it away.

Be a Person of Love to Give It Away

Jesus, in the Sermon on the Mount, gave concrete examples of what a person of love would do (turn the other cheek, love your enemy, bless those who curse you, etc.) Paul described what love *is* (patient, kind, etc.). We're called to *be* the manifestation of God's love. People ready to love patiently and kindly, without boasting or pride. People ready to keep no record of wrongs. God turns us into people of love. Then, when we encounter a situation which requires love, we naturally give it.

Larry—the most joyful person I know—is a wonderful example of this. He's a walking billboard for Jesus through his internal warmth. It's present in his face, warm smile, and the bear hugs he gives when he sees you. It's in his attentiveness, thoughtful questions, and heartfelt prayers. Larry gives away who he is, because he lives with the Kingdom's logic: *the more you give, the more you get.*[302] God's love travels to, and through, Larry. He is a person of love. As he gives it away, God fills him with *more*.

It's Okay To Rest and Recover

Be a person of love to give it away—what a simple idea.

But what if you're in a bad place? When I miss sleep, overwork, and live at a frenetic pace, I can't care well for others. Has a sleep-deprived, overworked, and anxious person running 15 minutes late ever slowed down to let you merge on the highway? It just doesn't work like that. Dallas Willard called hurry the great enemy of spiritual life in our day. He was right—we cannot be both loving and hurried.

There are other times, due to no fault of our own, we're in a space of unhealth. A light example of this is stubbing a toe. I do this *constantly*—it's a running joke in our house. "There goes dad on the floor; garbage can wins again." If I manage to avoid stubbing my toe, I'll step on a Lego for good measure. In any event, when we enter a place of pain, we can't think of anything else. We can't feel other feelings, think other thoughts, or have empathy for others.

There are times to dial back our pace. Cancer. Death. Sickness. A newborn. There's a long list. We can still pursue being people who would love, but we need to get over the guilt of feeling like we're disappointing God by resting and recovering. A Rule of Life must be flexible and adaptable to the season of life. God's not a task-master like Pharaoh, and we aren't workers with a quota of bricks. Loving our neighbor is not a forced behavior— it's a healthy overflow. In the unforced rhythms of grace, as we receive God's love, he brings us back to a place of rest.

Many new members at our church feel guilty for not immediately serving or volunteering. They understand a church—the body of Christ—needs everyone to carry weight. But often, they're hurting. They're coming to us in a season of depression, abuse, isolation, divorce, church hurt, and so on. As I listen, it becomes apparent they're in a *season* of pain. My encouragement is to lean into *healing*, not *doing*. If we do too much while in pain, we burn out and become bitter. We may even grow to resent God. This isn't right. God wants to care for us, bring us to a place of rest, and restore us—not sap us dry. He isn't the one making us serve in an unhealthy way.

In sports, an athlete discerns the *type* of injury by slowing down and listening to their body.

What caused it? Is it severe? Trying to run on a broken leg is not a smart move. When athletes avoid slowing down to see the doctor, they end up hurting themselves—irreparably at times.

On the flip side, while resting and healing are important, we also can't wait for *perfect* health to pursue our goal of loving others. If we have a sprained left toe (hey, this is no joke), we need to learn to push through.

> *He who watches the wind [waiting for all conditions to be perfect] will not sow [seed], and he who looks at the clouds will not reap [a harvest].*[303]

If we wait for the perfect circumstances to love our neighbor, we never will.

We need wisdom from above to know our internal temperature. God isn't a God of confusion.

> *If any of you lacks wisdom [to guide him through a decision or circumstance], he is to ask of [our benevolent] God, who gives to everyone generously and without rebuke or blame, and it will be given to him.*[304]

All this to say, to love your neighbor, self-assessment is necessary. As a pastor, at times I know I need to step back and recharge instead of rushing into more commitments to others. If you're in a season of pain, the best medicine is rest.

Let the physician of your soul, Jesus, guide the way into health—so you can love from the overflow of the heart.

And Who Is My Neighbor?

Have you ever over-complicated things and split hairs to get around what God clearly said? Me either…this hour.

In the first century, *this* (splitting hairs to get around God's teaching) happened when people debated whom to apply the "love your neighbor" teaching to. The same debate exists today. How is it splitting hairs? Underneath the question is a desire to get out of what Jesus calls us to do. We secretly want the definition of "neighbor" to be narrow because we see certain people as worthy of love (i.e., easy to love) and others as unworthy (i.e., hard to love).

Who is my neighbor? And who is yours? Those in our family? Neighborhood? Church? City? Political affiliation? Country? Belief system? What about the lowest of the morally low— pedophiles? Terrorists? At some point, we distinguish between *neighbor* and *enemy*. Each of us has a line we draw at a different place, but we all have one. At some point of moral depravity or distance, we say "enough." Not them.

Certainly, there are some people we aren't to love, right? Well, no. If we're to be people of love who respond in love to our neighbor, we cannot turn our love on and off like a faucet, giving it only to those we think deserve it.

In the first century, in response to Jesus' teaching about loving your neighbor, his Jewish audience asked where they could draw the line. Did he mean love Jews in the neighborhood? Perhaps all Jews in Israel? There was no way he meant *everyone*—as in *non-Jewish* neighbors. They watered down Jesus' command by making it a geographical question—to what distance is my fellow Jew a neighbor? Jesus clarified "neighbor" wasn't a matter of distance, but of the heart. It's being a person of compassion.

Today, we see ourselves as more morally progressive than those who lived 2,000 years ago. We shout from the rooftops of social media to "love your neighbor." Driving around Portland, Oregon, you see bumper stickers and signs to this effect in almost every yard: "In this house, we love *everyone*."

But you can't love an abstract idea ("everyone"). "Everyone" is not a person, and love isn't just theoretical. Love is messy, up close, and personal—not sterilized and distant.

It's Tina and Joel, small group leaders at our church, bringing cups of cold water, food, blankets, propane, and encouragement to those sleeping on the street near our church, week after week, year after year.

It's our young adults group offering prayer, hot cocoa, and love on the corner of 82nd, where prostitution and shootings happen regularly.

It's Kerri, faithfully ministering with a cheerful smile to the women in the prison she works at, seeing her placement as a strategic way to advance Jesus' movement.

Merely holding ideas about love misses the point.

Jesus spoke bluntly and boldly into the disconnect between abstract ideals and concrete actions when an expert of the law asked:

Who is my neighbor?[305]

Jesus was highly intelligent, and he answered the narrow question with a story about the good Samaritan and ended with a question of his own: *Who was a neighbor?*

The rabbinic style of teaching is question-based. When asked a question, it's common for a rabbi to respond with another instead of a direct answer. When Jesus ended the story of the good Samaritan with a question—*who proved to be a neighbor to the injured man?*—that was the answer.

"Proved" in Greek is *ginomai,* which is about *becoming* the kind of person who would love a neighbor.[306] Jesus' call is deeper than *believing* and even *doing* the right thing, it's about *becoming* a person of love.

Most of us know the story. A man traveled from Jerusalem to Jericho. The trip is a 14-mile hike down a *narrow* dirt path. The descent is 3,300 feet. This arduous trek takes the good part of a day. Jesus gave no specifics about the traveler: age, race, religion, or citizenship. The only thing we know is he was alone. Jesus' audience immediately picked up on the danger he was in.

The rocky terrain between Jerusalem and Jericho was a perfect place for bandits to hide, attack lone travelers, and flee into the desert.[307] Robbers knew people traveling to and from Jerusalem carried valuable goods (people often brought offerings to Jerusalem). Sure enough, in Jesus' story, thieves attacked the lone traveler, taking his clothes and leaving him for dead. The man had no food, water, or shelter. Completely exposed to the elements, it was only a matter of time before he died. The situation was dire.

Then, a priest and a Levite (religious officials) approached. They were either traveling to Jerusalem to give an offering or returning from it after performing their religious duties. Given their roles, the urgency of the situation, and the narrow trail, Jesus' story shows the callousness of their "belief-only" faith and failure to stop. They practically stepped over a dying man to get on with their "religion."

After they left, a Samaritan approached.

At the time, the divide between Jews and Samaritans was vast. You couldn't find two groups who despised each other more, with the feud going back hundreds of years. The reasons for the animosity were complex, but the result was the two groups had nothing to do with each other. They didn't live in the same places, intermarry, or interact. Many Jews traveled *around* Samaria so as to not set foot on Samaritan soil. They saw Samaritans as "half-breeds"—part Jewish and part pagan. Originally Jewish, the Samaritans intermarried with other cultures and adopted their practices. The Jews in turn frowned upon this and saw themselves as "better than" the Samaritans.

To *attempt* to find a modern example, think about how the most progressive Democrat feels about the most conservative

Republican. Imagine that multiplied by 500 years, and the divide being ethnic, not political, and you start to get *close* to the tension the audience felt as they heard the words "the Samaritan approached" leave Jesus' lips.

The Samaritan saw the wounded man, felt compassion, stopped, and cared for him. He carried the man to shelter (miles away) on his donkey. He fed, clothed, and financially supported his recovery. Simply put, his compassion moved him to treat the man as a human being.

The Jewish audience was shocked to hear the Samaritan was the hero of the story. Jesus challenged the box they put "others" in by placing one at the center of the story. Again, he concluded with a simple question:

Who was a neighbor to the injured man?

You could hear a pin drop as the audience sat and grappled with the implications. The expert finally forced the words out of pursed lips:

The one who had mercy on him.

Jesus closed his teaching:

Go and do the same.[308]

God isn't interested in how complicated we make things. The point is simple: the limitations we put on "neighbor"—and love—must go. There are only *neighbors*. This is convicting.

I've passed people with deep needs on my way to church many times. There are groups I've put in boxes who I have an extremely hard time loving. If I'm honest, I want them to suffer and face God's wrath, not receive love. Jonah felt the same way about the people of Nineveh.

But justice isn't ours to deliver. We don't get to be hair-splitting, calloused, religious observers stepping over people to perform rituals. John wrote:

> This is how we've come to understand and experience love: Christ sacrificed his life for us. This is why we ought to live sacrificially for our fellow believers, and not just be out for ourselves.[309]

Jesus is our good Samaritan. He came in our need and didn't pass us by. While the "righteous" stepped over us, he said:

> It is not the healthy who need a doctor, but the sick. I have not come to call the righteous, but sinners to repentance.[310]

We were the injured traveler dying on the side of the road. Without Jesus, we'd still be there. He rescued us out of sheer grace. We didn't *earn* his help and others don't *earn* ours. We love freely, as Jesus loved.

In his last address to his disciples, he said:

> 'And so I am giving a new commandment to you now—love each other just as much as I love you. Your strong love for each other will prove to the world that you are my disciples.'[311]

If you were in court with God as the judge and the enemy accused you of not being an apprentice of Jesus, the primary evidence would be how you treat other people. *This* is your greatest sermon.

WHEN HELPING HURTS

Let's take this conversation a step further. We're committed to love our neighbor and ready to respond—so, how do we actually do it? We don't want to ignore people like the religious officials. But we also don't want our help to hurt.

We don't help by doing everything people *want*, but by discerning and offering to meet their *needs*. Wisdom allows us to assess situations on a case-by-case basis. The woman at the well *wanted* water (a temporary solution), but *needed* living water. The man lame from birth outside the temple *wanted* money, but Peter met his *need*—healing.[312]

Further, even when we discern a need, it's not helpful to meet it *if* we'd be enabling the recipient. Enabling isn't loving. What if the traveler in Jesus' story wasn't injured but lying on the ground refusing to work? One could argue we shouldn't require people to earn our love, which is true. We didn't earn God's love, and others don't have to earn ours. However, it's not *loving* to encourage laziness. Throughout Proverbs, it's clear God isn't a fan of sluggards. Paul dealt with people who refused to work directly:

The one who is unwilling to work won't eat.[313]

All this to say, discernment from the Holy Spirit allows us to know when to step up and when to step back. Sometimes allowing natural consequences to happen is the most loving thing to do. The nuance of daily life is why we must walk in step with the Spirit and others. Discernment is "the faculty of discerning; discrimination; acuteness of judgment and understanding."[314] At its core, it's God helping us reach the best decision with the information we have. The Latin root of "discernment" means to "separate" or "set apart."[315] God gives us sharpened minds to separate good from best and truth from half-truth. If we do our utmost to listen for God's guidance and walk in the Spirit, making a best effort in the right direction is all we can do.

We must have *thick skin* but *soft hearts*.

Without discernment, our help sets people back instead of pushing them forward. Jesus assumes we will use discernment but warns to avoid thinking of ourselves as "better than" when we do.[316]

> *For in the same way you judge others, you will be judged, and with the measure you use, it will be measured to you.[317]*

Fairness and grace act as our true north on the moral compass. Sometimes, we misjudge or mishear God and help when we shouldn't, but it's better to err on the side of generosity, not scarcity. Religion is calloused, splitting hairs and looking for ways *out*. Jesus' love is reckless, looking for ways *in*.

SHAKING HANDS WITH
THE ENEMY

Let's add another layer to loving others: being people who would love our *enemies*.

Corrie Ten Boom was a Dutch Christian who helped Jews escape Nazi persecution during World War II. During the war, Nazis arrested her and her sister, Betsie, for concealing Jews in their Holland home. They sent them to a concentration camp, where Betsie died. In 1947, right after the war, Corrie gave a speech on forgiveness at a church in Munich, Germany. After the crowd dispersed a man in civilian clothing came forward. As he approached, she recognized him as one of the guards from the concentration camp. She recalled in an interview 25 years later:

> *Now he was in front of me, hand thrust out: "A fine message, fräulein! How good it is to know that, as you say, all our sins are at the bottom of the sea!" And I, who had spoken so glibly of forgiveness, fumbled in my pocketbook rather than take that hand…"You mentioned Ravensbrück in your talk," he was saying. "I was a guard in there." No, he did not remember me. "But since that time," he went on, "I have become a Christian. I know that God has forgiven me for the cruel things I did there, but I would like to hear it from your lips as well. Fräulein"– again the hand came out–"will you forgive me?"…It could not have been many seconds that he stood there, hand held out, but to me it seemed hours as I wrestled with the most difficult thing*

I had ever had to do... "Jesus, help me!" I prayed silently. "I can lift my hand. I can do that much. You supply the feeling." And so woodenly, mechanically, I thrust my hand into the one stretched out to me. And as I did, an incredible thing took place. The current started in my shoulder, raced down my arm, sprang into our joined hands. And then this healing warmth seemed to flood my whole being, bringing tears to my eyes. "I forgive you, brother!" I cried. "With all my heart!" For a long moment we grasped each other's hands, the former guard and the former prisoner. I had never known God's love so intensely as I did then.[318]

This story makes the heart pound with the tragedy and beauty of the moment. Loving a nice person is one thing, but what about a Nazi guard responsible for the death of your sister?

Jesus addressed loving our enemies head-on in the most famous speech of all time: the Sermon on the Mount:

You have heard that it was said, 'Love your neighbor and hate your enemy.' But I tell you, love your enemies and pray for those who persecute you, that you may be children of your Father in heaven.[319]

Many—including myself—have treated this as an expression, not a command. But we come to truly know Jesus when we can see him in the face of our adversary.

There will always be enemies. Two thousand years ago, they were the Romans and the morally corrupt (Samaritans, sex workers, and either zealots or tax collectors, depending on where you stood politically). Now, while social norms are different, it remains for many the government and the morally reprehensible (murderers, terrorists, pedophiles, Democrats or Republicans, etc.).

Why did Jesus teach *this*? He could have told us *not to harm* our enemies, but he calls us to *do good* to them. I don't know about you, but that's a hard pill to swallow. He's telling us to do something impossible apart from him. Perhaps that's the point. To love an enemy, we really need to be empowered by Jesus. It's like telling my seven-year-old son to fix the transmission— in a roundabout way, it's asking him to ask me for help.

To do the impossible things Jesus commands, we have to do them with him (relying on the Holy Spirit to empower us). When we do, we show the world we're different. Jesus' way is a life of love. When people see it, it begs the question: *What is so different about you?* If Jesus only gave us easy things to do, we'd just do them. Love puppies and nice people? Check and check. We wouldn't need him, and the world wouldn't see God through us. In a roundabout way, impossible things are exactly what we should be doing.

God's Kind of Love

What did Jesus mean by *love our enemies*? If we go back to the original Greek, we see it clearly. In English, one word has many different meanings. For instance, "love." "I *love* Taco Tuesday," "I *love* basketball," and "I *love* my son." Same word, different depth. In Greek, there is a specific word for each depth of love: *eros, phileo,* and *agapao.*

Eros is passionate love. It describes sexual attraction. It's the root of the word "erotic." A speaker uses "eros" to describe intense romantic love. It's based on a feeling someone evokes in you. However, when they no longer give you that feeling, the love is gone. In this way, eros is fleeting. It's here one day, gone the next. It's also transactional, in that we love people based on what they do for us. We don't love them as they are; we love them for what they provide. Jesus never *once* used eros to describe love.

Phileo is brotherly love. Think Philadelphia (the city of brotherly love) and philanthropy (the love of humankind). It's a higher form of love than eros in that it describes devotion deeper than feelings. Brotherly love is deep, but ultimately, voluntary. Either person can leave—there isn't a duty or covenant keeping them together. This isn't the type of love Jesus described either.

The word he did use (here and frequently) was *agape*. Agape is the highest form of love. It's not feelings-based (like eros) or voluntary (like phileo). It's unending and unconditional. It's the love a parent has for their child, a husband for his wife. It's eternal—it never ends. It's without agenda or strings attached—there's nothing the other person could do to earn or lose it. And it's dutiful—you do it whether you feel like it or not.

When Jesus says to love our enemy, he isn't proposing we manifest a romantic or sexual feeling (eros) or be best friends (phileo). He's calling us to pursue others without condition or expectation. This is God's love for the prodigal son. The world is full of eros and phileo, but agape is rare.

Agape does something to us, our enemies, and people witnessing it. It reconciles a fracture in humanity that started with Adam and Eve. It draws us together and closer to God. It's the most intense experience of God's love we'll ever have.

God's unconditional love will puncture the hardest heart, but it costs us *control*.

Our feelings no longer dictate who we love—Jesus does. That's scary. Who might Jesus ask you to love if you gave him control? Who in your life is discarded and discounted? Who needs his agape love? This is where God's Kingdom breaks through—practicing radical love. Agape love rattles the gates of hell.

> But I tell you, love your enemies **and pray** for those who persecute you....[320]

Opening our lips to pray for our persecutors is powerful. It expands the capacity of our hearts. As the words leave our mouth, God's warmth and love enter us in a new way. Thomas Merton said it like this:

> Love seeks one thing only: the good of the one loved.[321]

In this sense then, prayer orients our hearts toward seeking the good of our enemies.

In the end, agape love is freeing for everyone involved and simultaneously impossible without the continual presence of Jesus guiding the way. If we want to find Jesus, we should pray for opportunities to give agape love. Fortunately, they need not be grandiose. We can start here and now with those nearest to us. Jesus knows it's hard.

> We don't have a priest who is out of touch with our reality. He's been through weakness and testing, experienced it all—all but the sin.[322]

As nails pierced his hands and feet, back burning from 39 lashes, he brought us to mind and prayed for our forgiveness. May we have the grace to go and do the same.

SHEEP, GOATS, AND RESTORATIVE ACTS OF JUSTICE

As Fred Rogers lay on his deathbed, he asked one question to his wife, Joanne:

> Was I a sheep?

She gently replied:

> Yes, Fred, if there ever was a sheep, it was you. [323]

Why ask this as death knocked on his door? He knew it was *the* question he was about to answer before God.

Not to get too heavy, but let's go there. God holds us accountable for what we do, and don't do, in life. Jesus said when he returns, God will sort people into two categories: *sheep* and *goats*. My friend Ben, who works on a farm, dropped some knowledge on me about the difference between the two. While they look similar, sheep are naturally dependent on a shepherd while goats are highly independent.

It's been said sheep follow the shepherd, while goatherds follow the goat. Jesus said God welcomes the sheep (those willing to be led) into eternal life, while the goats (those who lead themselves) walk into exactly what they desire: eternal separation from God. According to Jesus, the dividing line between sheep and goats is action:

> For I was hungry and you gave me something to eat, I was thirsty and you gave me something to drink, I was a stranger and you invited me in, I needed clothes and you clothed me, I was sick and you looked after me, I was in prison and you came to visit me.' "Then the righteous will answer him, 'Lord, when did we see you hungry and feed you, or thirsty and give you something to drink? When did we see you a stranger and invite you in, or needing clothes and clothe you? When did we see you sick or in prison and go to visit you?' "The King will reply, 'Truly I tell you, whatever you did for one of the least of these brothers and sisters of mine, you did for me.'[324]

Jesus lists five restorative acts of justice—things that a person of love is poised to do. They feed the hungry, give the thirsty something to drink, practice hospitality with the stranger, clothe the naked, and visit the prisoner. When we follow the promptings of the Spirit and allow God to lead us to serve others, we serve Jesus. When we follow our own way and step over others, we do that to Jesus too.

What we do and don't do is personal to God. After Saul persecuted and murdered followers of The Way, Jesus knocked him down on the Damascus Road and said:

*Why are you doing this to **me**?*[325]

It's a sobering thought. Everything we do to *anyone*, we're doing to *Jesus.* Every person we pass by, degrade, look down on, and gossip about is Jesus. We aren't dealing with the barista, beggar, sex worker, immigrant, or enemy—we're dealing with Jesus. What life boils down to is how we treat others, because it's an indication of whether we followed God and put Jesus' words into practice. That's all that matters in the end.

THE CIRCLES OF LIFE: HOW WE GATHER

The aim of section four is to bring us from the abstract concept of love to the practice of it. The good news is we have hundreds of opportunities daily to *practice* loving God and neighbor. Remember, everything we do does something to us. Through small acts of kindness and love, we become more and more like our Teacher.

Jesus encountered people from vastly different walks of life—friends, rabbis, sex workers, Roman soldiers, etc. He loved each the same, yet treated people differently. He invested his time and energy primarily with 12 apprentices. As we start to talk about building communal practices into our Rule of Life—in both small and large settings—we'll start small with those in the inner circle of our social network.

Immediate Social Network

Robin Dunbar, Professor of Evolutionary Psychology at Oxford, studied relationships for decades. His findings form the modern understanding of "social networks." Like a spider web, a person's social network consists of every relationship they have, from close friends to distant relatives.

Through decades of research, Dunbar found our social networks have a ceiling. In other words, we have a limited capacity for the amount of relationships we can maintain.[326] As a rule of thumb, that figure, known as "Dunbar's number," is 150. We can only have 150 relationships at any given point in time.

Relationships require energy, time, laughter, touch, and a shared meal. With these ingredients present, intimacy increases; without, it grows cold. There's no such thing as treading relational water. Every relationship is either growing or dying based on time and energy invested. Close relationships require a high level of interaction. Author Helen Thompson says it takes 50 hours with someone to become a casual acquaintance, 90 to become a friend, and 200 to become a close friend.[327]

Here's the rub: we must choose who to invest in.

We each have 24 hours a day. We may not realize it, but investing in relationships A, B, and C necessarily means we can't do the same with relationships D, E, and F. All this to say, loving everyone the same cannot mean treating everyone the same. We can't invest in everyone *equally*. Jesus didn't.

Dunbar's studies found different relational circles naturally form within the 150. These groups are concentric circles of 50 (good friends), 15 (close friends), five (best friends), and one (life partner). The smaller the group, the greater the intimacy.

Throughout history, people gathered in "tribes" of 150. We see this in early hunter-gatherer societies, small villages, and more recently, industrialized societies. Now, offices, factories, residential campsites, military organizations—even Christmas card lists are 150 strong. Your "tribe" is the group you'd invite to a wedding, graduation, or funeral. Tribes naturally form based on family lines, lineage, and location. Generally, if the group exceeds 150 it's unlikely to last.[328] It's too big. Many startups that grow beyond 150 begin to notice they're too large and rigid. At this size, interactions and intimacy cannot be deep with everyone.

Within a tribe, there are 35 to 50 "good friends." Before you spit out your coffee because "who has the time for 50 good friends?" let me tell you what Dunbar means. This is the group of people within our tribe we socialize with more frequently. The intimacy level is higher, but still not very deep. "Good friends" are the people you'd invite to a barbecue, Christmas party, or semi-annual event—if you did that kind of thing.

Within the "good friends," there's a smaller group of 12 to 15 "close friends." These are the people we do life with. Groups of this size are cohesive, work well together, and allow for intimacy, conversation, and connection. Historically, this is why the Romans arranged their army into nine-man *contuberniums* and the Greeks had 8-to 16-man *stichos*.[329] Sports teams also generally stick to a small group of 12-15 players on the field.

Within this group, there's a smaller circle of three to five "best friends." These are the people we naturally gravitate toward, mutually keep up with, and converse easily and frequently with. Among our close friends, one (maybe two) are our confidants and deepest relationships. This is likely a romantic partner and/or best friend. We see these concentric circles in Paul's life. He had a select group of seven apprentices: Barnabas, Silas, Luke, John Mark, Apollos, Timothy, and Titus. Of the seven, he was closest with two, Timothy and Titus (his "sons").[330]

Why does this matter? This isn't a sociology class or an effort to make ourselves cry because we don't have as many friends as Dunbar says we should. This is the framework by which we're going to approach the practice of doing life together in a small community group.

Cultural Sidebar

Allow me to further set up the idea of communal practices with a brief examination of the "warm" culture in which they happen. Jesus lived in a welcoming and community-minded culture in the Middle East. America is a cold and individual culture in the West. The contrast could not be sharper. In a warm culture, the individual exists for the community. The purpose of life isn't individual success; it's contributing to the larger group. In a cold culture, the community exists for the individual. It's all about individual rights and rugged individualism, heroizing those who "pulled themselves up by their bootstraps."

The difference in cultures extends to how we view the home. In America, we say: "A man's home is his castle." Our mindset is that homes are places of retreat to keep the world out. In a warm culture, the mindset is: "Mi casa es su casa"—my house is your house. The home is a place to host and welcome others into.

Our perspectives shape how we live. In a cold culture, dinner exists for the function of ingesting food. It's often rushed, and when the food is gone, so are the people. In a warm culture, the point of dinner is connection and conversation. Gatherings around the table are sacred and unhurried. *Sobremesa*, a Spanish term—encapsulates this concept well. It's the practice of enjoying good food, meaningful conversation, and time with each other well after the final dish is served. In Latin America (and many European, Mediterranean, Asian, and Arabic cultures), sobremesa is a way of life.

Jesus was born and raised in a warm culture. His way of life was sobremesa, not "my home is my castle." His teachings contain a culture shift for many of us—like myself—born and raised in a cold environment. As we talk about community and

Jesus' way of doing life together, we should appreciate this is new for many of us and flips cold culture on its head. Jesus did life in community and ministry around a table. In Luke's recording of Jesus' ministry, we see him ministering in three main places: walking to dinner, talking at dinner, or leaving dinner. He practiced life at the table.

When he said he came to give life and life to the full, *this* is what he was talking about.[331]

Life together.

Jesus' Social Network

Jesus' relationships fit neatly into Dunbar's concentric circles. He had thousands in the crowds, hundreds of disciples, 72 good friends, 12 close friends, three best friends, and one closer than the rest. How do we know this? He appeared to over 500 followers after God raised him from the dead.[332] There were 120 in the upper room (those 120 showed a high level of dedication to Jesus by waiting 50 days for the Holy Spirit to come).[333] He called 72 disciples to travel and share his message.[334] And he did life with 12 apprentices for three years on a deeper level.

It's no coincidence he chose 12—not 120—as his core group. He knew effective apprenticeship couldn't be a mile wide and an inch deep. He had limited time and wanted to deeply form the small group into an empowered, cohesive, and equipped force to adopt his way of life (his "yoke") and spread his message. His invitation was simple: do life with me.

They walked, ate, watched, learned, wrote, prayed, celebrated, and mourned together. They experienced every aspect of life *with* Jesus.

Among the 12, he had three intimate relationships (Peter, John, and James). Of the three, Peter was arguably his closest friend, as Jesus disclosed more to him than anyone else.[335] In three portions of Scripture, we see a distinction between the 12 and the three. First, Jesus allowed only Peter, John, and James to watch as he resurrected a little girl. He directed them to tell no one (including the other nine).[336] He showed them he had absolute power over death, a truth that was invaluable later as they grappled with his crucifixion. Second, he had only Peter, John, and James watch his transfiguration into a glorified state. Again, he directed them to tell no one.[337] He wanted them to grasp who he was. Perhaps this is why Peter was so bold as he gave his speeches (captured in the book of Acts): he knew *who* Jesus was. Finally, in Gethsemane—a park Jesus frequented—he asked Peter, James and John to be with him as he prayed. He invited them into a vulnerable, painful, and intense moment in his life simply because he wanted them there.

It's incredible, 2,000 years later, to see the exponential impact of his intentionality with 12 individuals. Peter, James, and John became key leaders in the early church, and the disciples spread his message throughout the world. Through them, God turned 120 in the upper room into over 2.6 billion followers today. Statisticians project the number to increase to 3.3 billion by 2050.[338]

PRACTICE: GATHERING IN SMALL COMMUNITIES

We see from the life of Jesus the importance of sharing our fire with an inner circle. His Rule of Life was to gather frequently with a small group of people. This is a lost practice for many of us in today's world. Our first step in the direction of life in community is to recognize it doesn't just happen. No one else will form or maintain a community for us. We must be the initiators to gather and prioritize a group of people to follow Jesus with.

While larger gatherings—whether 20 or 2,000—are powerful reminders we exist as part of a larger faith community, smaller groups are where we grow.

For Trees and People, Community Is Life or Death.

In *The Hidden Life of Trees*, Peter Wohlleben explores the amazing life of trees, which share many similarities to humans (as we've discussed above). Wohlleben's decades-long studies showed isolated trees are the weakest because they have no support system when they get sick, infected, or compromised. When storms hit, they have no trees around to buffer the impact. On the other hand, trees that grow in "tree families," a group of trees that live together, are the strongest. These tree families share resources through an interconnected underground root network. When one gets sick, infected, or compromised, the others all send nutrients through the network to help it recover, as they understand the importance of each community member.

In tree families, big trees help small trees grow by towering over them and taking up most of the sunlight. While this isn't intuitive—less sun seems *bad* for the small trees underneath—it's actually *good*. As the big tree covers them, they get resourceful. They're forced to grow a deep root system to get water and in turn develop a wide trunk. If the big tree falls before the smaller trees are developed, they get too much sun, too quickly. They shoot up without the root system or trunk to support the rapid growth. And skinny and unrooted trees don't withstand the storms. However, when the small tree gets the full covering of the big tree for five to ten years, its roots grow deep and its trunk grows wide. Then, when the larger tree naturally bows out, the smaller one rises and begins to cover those below it. That's the circle of life with trees, and it's also true for humans.

We're stronger when we do life together.

While we think we can grow tall alone (perhaps via influence and power), community keeps us grounded. Our culture is inundated with countless examples of isolated leaders getting a platform which outpaces their character—and then they fall. Community strengthens our rootedness and allows us to grow under the protection of wise friends. In God's timeline, we eventually become big trees to others. We deeply want this type of life.

To reorient our lives around Jesus' vision of community is not a new concept. It requires opening our homes during the week, sharing meals, praying, and building relationships over a lifetime. This is how the early followers of Jesus lived (see Acts 2v42-47). They ate together, prayed, and lived in deep relationship with one another. They had their individual practices, but they also followed a shared Rule of Life.

What It Can Look Like

Consider what this can look like for you. Who are five to 12 people you already know who you could start a group with? Consider gathering weekly on a set day in a home (yours or a group member's) for two hours. During the first hour, share a potluck meal and catch up with everyone. This can be organic or using a prompt ("share your onion and rose"—that is, the best and worst thing that happened this week). Once everyone has caught up, take 45 minutes to work through a guided discussion with a conversation facilitator.

Consider working through how to apply last Sunday's sermon or focusing on a particular practice.[339] Then, during the last 15 minutes, go around the group and share prayer requests. Have someone take notes and share them in the group chat (to check in with the person next week), and pray as a group.

This sounds radically ordinary. (It is.)

However, consistency and commitment will turn this small group into an incredibly formative experience for everyone.

Building a Shared Rule of Life

As you're practicing a Rule of Life, you can also build in communal practices with your group. Most of the individual practices can also be done with others. For instance, prayer is both an individual *and* communal practice. It can be communal by praying together and interceding for each other. (Have a group chat going throughout the week where prayer requests are shared.) Further, you can practice a shared daily rhythm: pray the Lord's Prayer each morning, in the afternoon pray for the lost, and pray reflectively with gratitude in the evening (daily office).

You can fast together, picking a regular day and time. Participate in a shared Scripture reading plan, which is easy to do on YouVersion. Serve together in church one Sunday a month, and sit together the other Sundays. Pick a community project and do that instead of meeting in a home one of the weeks of the month. And have fun together! By practicing your faith collectively, God will weave your lives together, forming a beautiful and interconnected tapestry.

Making Interpersonal Relationships Work

We know deep, Christ-centered relationships are important, but how can we form them in the modern era? Simple: live intentionally with a framework and plan of action.

Carey Nieuwhof said nobody asks us to accomplish *our* highest priorities; they ask us to accomplish *theirs*.[340] It's not malicious, but everything and everyone outside your inner circle will ask for your time and energy. C.S. Lewis observed:

When we put first things first, we get first things and second things are thrown in. But when we put second things first, we lose both first and second things.[341]

If Jesus said yes to everything, he would have in turn said no to deep discipleship with the 12. But he was keenly focused on investing and building into them, and he didn't allow himself to be distracted from his primary mission by the myriad of other forces at play.

According to *Psychology Today*, we make an average of 35,000 decisions daily. This means we make a decision every two seconds, sunup to sundown.[342] From the moment we wake, we're deciding: what to wear, what to eat for breakfast, when to leave. Again, if we don't plan ahead and build in a Rule of Life for community in small settings, it won't happen. We'll get sucked up by the immediate to the detriment of the important.

When faced with *any* relational decision, first identify the *type* of relationship it is. Where does it fall in your concentric circles—150, 50, 15, five, or one? To do this, be honest about what *is* and not what it *could be*. The idea is to invest the first-fruits of your time and energy into your innermost circle.

Roseanne and I label relationships as "ones" through "fours" based on Dunbar's concentric circles. We're not *ranking* or *judging*. A label (along with pre-decisions for that label) simply helps us decide what to say yes to and what to say no to. With four young kids, our time and energy are *limited*. We want to make as many pre-decisions as possible to root ourselves in an intentional community.

We want to invest our best into our "ones" and "twos." My "ones" are Roseanne and the kids. "Twos" are our circle of 12 to 15. These include parents, spiritual fathers and mothers, close friends, and family. "Threes" are friends (the circle of 50), and "fours" are acquaintances (the circle of 150).

With ones, we pre-commit to give the best of our time and energy, along with full access to our lives. With twos, it's similar, but not to the same extent. For twos, we've set aside Tuesday and Wednesday evenings to share a meal, check in, and have meaningful conversations. Tuesday nights we meet with our community group (see structure above). On Wednesday nights, we gather with our family. Friday evenings (once a month) are for hosting and inviting new friends (threes) to our table. This is what works for *us*, in this season. It's different with every family and season of life. The point I'm making isn't to follow our specific regimen, but to be intentional to plan *frequent* time with ones and twos.

If there's a conflict, I've pre-planned to choose my ones. Anyone with healthy boundaries respects and understands when you need to step back to make sure your ones are getting what they need. This pre-decision, for me, has been a game-changer. For years, I spread myself too thin trying to do everything to please everyone. It wasn't anyone's fault but my own. I didn't realize by saying yes to everything, I was saying no to the most important things. Making on-the-fly relational decisions without a framework—a Rule of Life—is exhausting. Even more importantly, you'll neglect your ones and twos for less important relationships.

Along with our built-in community nights, Roseanne and I go on a weekly date. This past month, the kids were sick, our parents were traveling, and we went on one date instead of four. These kinds of months happen. The point of building a Rule of Life is that—like an anchor—it keeps us from drifting too far. When we start to feel the tug of an anchor—when we're out of rhythm—we slow down and address it.

Any relationship outside of your inner circle is by default either a three or four. It's not a knock on anyone, it simply acknowledges they aren't your spouse, child, parent, or close friend. Level three relationships are likely coworkers, friends, and extended family. We maintain such relationships through more infrequent gatherings, like coffee, lunch, weekend get-togethers, and church.

These relationships are great. They can even grow deeper if we invest more into them. However, it's important to see what *is*. Threes aren't ones or twos, and shouldn't get the same energy. This is challenging if you have a big heart. As a rule of thumb, relating with threes takes more time. There's scheduling, traveling to meet in a formal setting (restaurant, coffee shop, or other neutral venue), and energy as we're more "on" than with our ones and twos. We need to go into interactions with threes with a clear understanding of what we have to give.

Author Lysa TerKeurst, who wrote *Good Boundaries and Goodbyes*, suggests we provide *access* to our lives proportionate to the level of responsibility the other person has shown.[343] In other words, if a person has demonstrated little to no responsibility in your life, don't feel pressured to give a high level of access. Jesus interacted with threes and fours but didn't spend disproportionate time and energy there.

Once you label the relationship, slow down and think about each commitment you make, *before you make it*. It takes *time* and *space* to honestly assess what you have to give. Think about your prior commitments, how your ones are doing, and how much time and energy you have to *happily* give—if any. When we make spontaneous commitments, we can't consider these factors. It's better to step back and look at the big picture beforehand. "Let me check my calendar and get back to you" isn't rude; it's wise.

Sometimes the answer is no, and that's okay. As a recovering people please-aholic, it's been a struggle to realize that when someone asks to spend time together, *I don't have to* say yes. Maybe I'm preaching to the choir, but my guess is we all struggle with this to some extent.

You're in control of who you see and how often you see them. If it doesn't work, you don't have to make it happen by bending your calendar and sacrificing prior commitments. It's perfectly fine to decline a request. There doesn't need to be a reason, and often, leaving the door open ("Let's circle back in a few weeks") isn't the right answer. If you get strong pushback when you say, "I don't have time," know you're dealing with a person lacking a healthy understanding of boundaries. Mature people respect healthy boundaries. They understand you have other commitments and limited time and energy, and it's not personal.

If you've thought it through and want to meet (whether on a recurring or one-time basis), determine what you can *happily* give. If it's an hour, communicate when you need to leave (either in the planning stage or when the get-together starts).

I had coffee with an old friend a few months ago. I was happy to do it and expected it would last an hour, but he had a very different idea of what "getting coffee" meant. An hour in, he was in the middle of a sensitive story, and it would have been inappropriate to say I had to leave. We had different frameworks, and I didn't communicate what I had to give. Have you ever been in a situation like this? We ended up spending *three hours* at coffee. I vented to Roseanne that evening about how this individual could be so self-centered, but she told me straight up: "You didn't communicate your boundary or speak up. That's on you."

I have to tell myself these concepts constantly: *I am responsible for developing appropriate boundaries. I am responsible for assessing my boundaries before I engage. I am responsible for communicating my boundaries. And I am responsible for sticking to my boundaries.* Had I communicated I only had an hour, I would've been well within my rights to leave and this individual would have likely approached our conversation differently.

Another consideration is travel time. It feels like we're getting into the weeds, but an hour-long coffee appointment across town isn't an hour—it's *two* if you include the drive. If you have an hour to give, aim to meet where you are or a place within five minutes. If coffee is at 11 and it's five minutes away, you're leaving at 10:45 and returning at 12:15—*90 minutes.* If you know upfront you have 90 minutes to give—go for it!

Another time-killer is scheduling. I've found Calendly (a free scheduling tool that allows people to select available time slots based on your calendar) saves about 10 back-and-forth messages. If a scheduling tool isn't your thing, consider this template:

"Hi John! I'd love to get together! Next week [picking a week that works for me], I have time between 11 and noon on Tuesday, Wednesday, or Friday. If that works for you, would [insert location close to you] work? If those times don't work, what about the following week on [insert another day and time]. If none of those work, I'll put in my calendar to circle back with you in three weeks and see if our calendars have opened up. Thanks so much!"

Respect your time and others will too.

A message like this cuts through the back-and-forth and gets something on the calendar. And if it doesn't work out, it doesn't work out. If a person at level three or beyond can't work with what you have to give, don't bend to what doesn't work for you.

When we ask someone to meet, remember they may not have the time or energy for the same reasons we don't. Therefore, giving recipients an easy "out" in the invitation is kind. We can end an invitation with: "I know things are likely busy, so if this doesn't work out, I completely understand!" We should aim to respect other people's boundaries as much as we want them to respect ours.

The Practice of Hosting Conversation

One of the most valuable and underutilized practices is hosting a conversation.

A primary way we can love our neighbor is through listening and asking good questions. David Brooks' book *How to Know a Person* is an incredible resource on this topic.[344] He defines a good conversation as a joint exploration and two-way exchange. Much like a river guide, you can help steer the conversation into meaningful waters to serve whomever you're interacting with.

Before any gathering, consider taking 60 seconds to pray for the individual or group. God's Spirit—via prayer—opens our hearts to others in a deep way. Before you meet, think of meaningful questions to ask. Think about their season of life, likes, and dislikes. Try to put yourself in their shoes *before* you step foot into the room. What might they be feeling, thinking, and experiencing? This will help you ask *mindful* questions.

The first part of any conversation—small talk—establishes trust. I once heard it takes seven minutes of small talk for a person to develop the psychological safety (i.e., trust) to share anything deeper. It's not something to skip over. You can ask about family, interests, school, or hobbies (remember the acronym FISH)—but the point is—be *curious*.

It's especially helpful to ask questions that provoke a story, not just yes-or-no answers. Brooks calls these "narrative-based" questions (i.e., they take people back in time to tell a story). This "take me back" technique, wherein you ask questions about a person's childhood and formative years, is powerful. ("Ah, so you grew up in Los Angeles. What was that like for you?") Any questions that invite a story, when you've shown genuine interest in the other person, will most likely be returned by them opening up and sharing. Through asking thoughtful questions and listening, you're building a bridge of trust you can drive deeper conversation across.

Brooks encourages us to be childlike in our questions (i.e., direct). Many of us stop asking honest questions over time as we begin to withdraw from intimacy. He says the average child asks 40,000 questions between the age of two and five! In the book, he shares about an experiment a teacher once did with eighth grade boys, in which she had them interview her and told them they could ask anything. Here's how the conversation went:

Boy 1: Are you married?
Teacher: No.
Boy 2: Are you divorced?
Teacher: Yes.
Boy 3: Do you still love him?
Teacher: [deep gasp]
Boy 4: Does he know you still love him? Does he know?
Teacher: [tears in eyes]
Boy 5: Do your children know?

Kids aren't afraid to ask. A good question helps others reach into themselves to answer. By observing body language and noticing what people light up about, we have a window into their soul. The aim is always to ask and listen more than we speak, as you've probably heard before. To put it another way: focus on being *interested*, not *interesting*.

Follow the "30-70 rule," which means talk 30 percent of the time and listen 70. Interestingly, asking good follow-up questions often requires pausing for longer than usual to truly listen to what was just said. Brooks notes in America, we're only comfortable with a four-second pause, while in Japan, they wait as long as eight seconds to reply. His encouragement: wait, pause, take an extra breath, and consider your response before speaking.

In *Celebration of Discipline*, Richard Foster writes about Peter's lack of listening skills. The scene is on a mountain, during Jesus' transfiguration. Jesus was in a deep conversation with Moses and Elijah. Peter was there too, watching. Then he jumped in:

> *Lord, it is good for us to be here. If you wish, I will put up three shelters—one for you, one for Moses and one for Elijah.*[345]

Listening is important—nobody was even talking to Peter!

If there is conversational depth, don't be afraid to ask big questions which serve the other person by helping them to reflect on the truth as they answer, such as:

What crossroads are you at? (At any moment most of us face some sort of transition.)
What would you do if you weren't afraid?
If you die tonight, what would you regret not doing?
If we meet a year from now, what will we be celebrating?
If the next five years are a chapter in your life, what is that chapter about?

Can you be yourself where you're at and still fit in?
What have you said yes to that you no longer believe in?[346]

If appropriate, ask if there's anything you can pray about. And if appropriate, pray then and there. Although this requires discretion, prayer is often *the* most powerful gift you can give.

Jesus with Threes and Fours

Jesus engaged threes and fours, like his interactions with the Pharisees and Sadducees. They often asked for his time, engaged in debates, tried to trap him, and even insulted him. He responded by sharing the truth, but he didn't drain himself with emotional vampires. He engaged to a certain extent but moved on when their ears and hearts remained closed. When Nicodemus asked for time, he made it. But he refused to be exhausted by others and kept a certain distance to protect himself, thereby fulfilling God's calling for his life.

He showed loving deeply and widely is possible while maintaining personal boundaries. He *deeply* loved all people. Entering Jerusalem for the last time, he looked over the city and spoke from his soul with a groan:

> *Jerusalem! Jerusalem! Murderer of prophets! Killer of the ones who brought you God's news! How often I've ached to embrace your children, the way a hen gathers her chicks under her wings, and you wouldn't let me.[347]*

He didn't impose himself on anyone. His method was invitation, not coercion, as John describes in Revelation:

[i]f anyone hears My voice and opens the door, I will come in and eat with him (restore him), and he with Me.[348]

Jesus taught his apprentices that when they engaged with others, they brought peace with them:

If someone who promotes peace is there, your peace will rest on them; if not, it will return to you.[349]

We don't need to force relationships to happen or strive to maintain more of these deep connections than we should. Instead, as we build a Rule of Life around loving our neighbor, we allow God's Spirit to lead us to the people of peace with whom we will do life.

UNITY IN COMMUNITY

The goal is for all of them to become one heart and mind—just as you, Father, are in me and I in you. - Jesus, John 17v20–23 (MSG)

Following Jesus is a team sport. Henri Nouwen once said:

God is the hub of the wheel of life. The closer we come to God the closer we come to each other. The basis of community is not primarily our ideas, feelings, and emotions about each other but our common search for God. When we keep our minds and hearts directed toward God, we will come more fully "together."[350]

Like individual spokes on a wheel, as we journey closer to God at the center, we necessarily grow closer to each other. This is by design.

Culturally—as we've discussed—we live in a cold environment. If we're not intentional, we'll drift into an individualized pursuit of God that consists of a series of things we do alone. To be blunt, if we do this, we've created a Western version of a communal faith. This isn't what Jesus intended.

It also isn't a new phenomenon. In the sixth century, St. Benedict addressed a growing group of followers who retreated to the desert to pursue Jesus individually because they were so fed up with the evil they saw in society. He emphasized the importance of relationships because he understood *deep inner formation only happens in Christ-centered communities.* It's only by being with others that we come to see our blind spots, pretensions, and rough edges. Community *exposes* us, and we grow as a result. It's in community that those who know us can encourage us to live up to our full potential and hold us accountable to pursue it.

In leaving church, many abandon the community they so desperately need. We all need a group of people to do life with, encourage us in our apprenticeship to Jesus, and lovingly challenge us. Real community is a sacred space where the love of God touches our reality.

Why are people retreating from local faith communities despite the rampant isolation they face outside of them? A decades-old quote from Gandhi may hold a piece of the answer:

I like your Christ. I do not like your Christians. Your Christians are so unlike your Christ.[351]

Ouch. But he's not wrong. People are turned off by the behavior of proclaimed followers of Jesus.

God sees what's happening in the Western church. The hypocrisy, religious nationalism, celebrity preacher culture, sexual abuse, and cruelty. It all must go. God *will* provide justice. But what do we do in the meantime? We should be careful to avoid standing on the sidelines criticizing every local faith community because a few are highlighted in the news. Sam Rayburn once said:

Anybody can kick down a barn, but it takes a good carpenter to build one.[352]

In the same vein, anybody can criticize the church, but it takes real courage to be willing to see the flaws in Jesus' bride and fight to make her better.

Jesus invites us to collectively follow him, and as we do, he makes *us* fishers of men.[353] Our potential is exponentially greater when we do life together. Many who left the church are returning, but to what? There needs to be a new commitment to building real community in the congregation. The future of the church is ancient—it's returning to this sacred way of doing life.

PRACTICE: GATHERING IN CHURCH

Along with an emphasis on smaller communities, it's important to build larger faith gatherings into your Rule of Life. Why? Because Jesus did. In his time, if you were a practicing Jew, you gathered weekly at the local synagogue. Sure, you visited the Temple in Jerusalem from time to time to celebrate larger occasions, but weekly synagogue was the bread and butter. "Synagogue" originates from the Greek *synagōgē*, meaning assembly.[354]

It's commonly believed the practice of gathering weekly began after the Jewish people were conquered and exiled to Babylon.[355] In a foreign, hostile, and dominant culture seeking to assimilate them and erase their way of life, they recognized the need to meet *frequently*. Gatherings arose out of necessity. If they didn't come together, they'd be erased by the dominant Babylonian culture.

When they returned to Israel, they continued the practice of gathering weekly and built synagogues in most towns and villages. Synagogues were the center of community life— more like a YMCA than a monastery. They were places for study, education, reflection, prayer, and worship. A few individuals managed the synagogue, and the community gathered once a week on Saturday (*Shabbat*, or Sabbath) to collectively worship.

The gathering was simple and beautiful.

It began with several blessings to God, followed by a collective recitation of the *Shema* (a prayer from Deuteronomy):

> *Hear, O Israel: The Lord our God, the Lord is one.*[356]

Different individuals took turns reading portions of the Torah (Genesis, Exodus, Leviticus, Numbers, and Deuteronomy), followed by the *Nevi'im* (Prophets). Afterward, an adult male in the faith community gave a brief sermon.[357] Finally, the service concluded with a blessing.

Jesus, a practicing Jew, attended synagogue weekly.[358] He spent lots of time there and performed miracles, including healings, in the synagogues.[359] We also know he followed God's will *perfectly.*[360] Therefore, we can infer his weekly rhythm of gathering with a local faith community is incredibly important. As only engaged members of the community were allowed to be on the speaking schedule, for Jesus to teach in a synagogue shows he was not only present, but also an engaged member of the larger community.[361] He said he came to fulfill the law, not depart from it. And he interpreted the law—the third commandment of practicing the Sabbath—to include worshiping God with other believers.[362] Jesus loved and honored the weekly gathering and impressed this practice on his early followers.

How We've Drifted

How did we get from *there* to *here*, where about one third of Christians attend church weekly?[363]

Why, when the weather is good or something else is scheduled on Sunday morning, do we neglect church? It's simply not a priority in our culture.

Contrast this with Jesus' early followers—devout Jews—who attended synagogue to the point of persecution. As they confessed Jesus, synagogue leaders began excommunicating them from both the weekly gatherings and the larger Jewish community.[364] The hostility from the Roman government also increased to the extent they had to go into hiding.[365] It was in this season many were persecuted, imprisoned, and martyred.[366] Excluded from the local synagogues, they formed house churches out of necessity.[367]

In those weekly gatherings, they modified—but did not discard—their Jewish roots. To the Jewish service, they added Jesus' instruction to break bread in remembrance of him (i.e., communion).[368] They practiced communion daily in the beginning.[369] They also changed the Sabbath from Saturday, when Jews met, to Sunday.[370] Why? Sunday was the first day of the week, representing giving God their first-fruits, and also the day Jesus rose from the dead. Gathering on Sunday is a way to remember and honor Jesus.[371]

The New Testament writers called these gatherings the *Ekklesia*. The historian Luke wrote that Barnabas and Saul met with the *Ekklesia* in Antioch.[372] Paul wrote that he formerly persecuted the *Ekklesia* of God.[373] Over time, as we translated Greek to English, this is how we got the word "church." The point is they still patterned the gatherings after the synagogue. In Jesus' time, every follower's Rule of Life included a frequent (daily and weekly) gathering involving worship, study, and prayer.[374]

The early followers of Jesus were not concerned with where they met, who was preaching that Sunday, or hype. Instead—operating under intense persecution—they focused on building a community which cared for one another and was completely centered around Jesus. They didn't just sing; they *worshiped*. They gathered wherever they could, whenever they could. This included doing church in homes, rented rooms, outside the temple, in schools, on beaches, and by rivers. The location didn't matter. Their faith was simple and pure.

If Paul wrote to the Western church today, he'd chide us for our obsession with buildings, emotionalism, disunity, and lack of love. We need to fight to maintain the simplicity and purity present in the early days. Now, many are more focused on going viral on Instagram than making space for the Holy Spirit to move. Paul intentionally kept it simple when he spoke at gatherings so the focus would be on God's Spirit and power, not him. In his first letter to the Corinthian church, he said:

> *You'll remember, friends, that when I first came to you to let you in on God's sheer genius, I didn't try to impress you with polished speeches and the latest philosophy. I deliberately kept it plain and simple: first Jesus and who he is; then Jesus and what he did—Jesus crucified....But the Message came through anyway. God's Spirit and God's power did it, which made it clear that your life of faith is a response to God's power, not to some fancy mental or emotional footwork by me or anyone else.*[375]

This was Paul's approach. The message of peace, coupled with God's Spirit, is more than enough. The power of a sermon lies not in its complexity or showmanship, but in its simplicity and dependence on the Holy Spirit. Richard Foster adds:

Heart preaching enflames the spirit of worship; head preaching smothers the glowing embers. There is nothing more quickening than spirit-inspired preaching, nothing more deadly than human-inspired preaching.[376]

From what I've seen, many modern preaching courses focus on technique (which is important) but neglect guidance on spiritual preparation (fasting, prayer in the Spirit, and desperation for the Holy Spirit to move).

Dietrich Bonhoeffer, one of the most heroic apprentices of Jesus, said:

Do not try to make the Bible relevant. Its relevance is axiomatic.... Do not defend God's Word but testify to it.... Trust in the Word. It is a ship loaded to the very limits of her capacity.[377]

If we water the Word down and don't preach on repentance and sin, we don't give God's Spirit a chance to convict. Bonhoeffer's approach was simple. He believed theatrics were unnecessary and even detrimental to conveying the Word. He did not feel "hype" was important. He said of his preaching style:

I do not give life to [the Word], but it gives life to me and to the congregation.... Only the unprepared preacher has to use the

techniques of emotionalism, shouting, or exercising influences
through pressure. These techniques betray his insecurity.[378]

We live in a culture that craves hype and a spiritual experience. The Church—using a "church growth model"—has not been immune to the pressure to produce and entertain. And if a church simply aims to provide the best service to attract the largest crowd, it's problematic.

Performance-driven gatherings work until they don't. If you make your living on performance, when you have an off week, people move on. In an issue of *Mission Frontiers*, Mike Breen writes that in the United States, *96 percent* of church growth is due to church hopping (i.e., people moving from one church to another).[379]

In Revelation, we see how Jesus evaluated churches. Of Laodicea, he said:

> *I know your deeds, that you are neither cold nor hot. I wish you were either one or the other! So, because you are lukewarm—neither hot nor cold—I am about to spit you out of my mouth...be earnest and repent.*[380]

If the Spirit is fire, it's polar opposite is coldness. Lukewarmness is neither fully Spirit-led or Spirit-less—it's a *maintaining* church. It's a church that goes through the motions, Sunday after Sunday. It may have a nice building, but it never makes a difference. It never invites the Spirit, serves the poor, prays in desperation, lives in fellowship, or reaches the lost. If that church disappeared tomorrow, the community wouldn't even notice. Wealth, building size, and attendance aren't how Jesus evaluates success. He didn't mention any of those things when assessing any of the seven churches in Revelation.

How did he evaluate churches? Here's what he said: Laodicea was lukewarm and wretched. Ephesus had doctrine but lacked love. Smyrna was spiritually rich and endured persecution. Pergamum held to Christ but also to false teaching. Thyatira was growing in love but tolerating heresy. Sardis was lifeless, as shown by their dead works. Philadelphia kept God's word and never denied Jesus.

Many have become distracted by church growth techniques and programs to the neglect of hosting God's Spirit. We don't want to be self-reliant on our abilities. God blesses gatherings of people who are humble and hungry for his presence.

Jesus said:

I will build my Ekklesia.[381]

It's his church, which he deeply cares about. Paul talked about this in his letter encouraging the Ephesian elders to:

...shepherd the church of God which he purchased with his own blood.[382]

Jesus made our gatherings possible through his sacrifice. And without his resurrection, there is no celebrating, preaching, or gathering—we should just pack it up and go home. But with his resurrection and offer of new life, our gatherings become of the utmost importance. If we understood the extent to which God cares about Sundays—the degree to which he takes joy in pure and unadulterated worship—we'd approach church differently. It would be less about program and performance and more about creating space for God's Spirit to move. It would truly be a house of prayer.[383]

We must open ourselves to God's Kingdom for that to happen.

The church, also known as the body of Christ, has much growing to do. Paul explained that only at the end of this age will it be presented to Christ in all its glory, without blemish.[384] So while the church will grow, God compels us to take an active role through large and small gatherings of believers. In the final section of this book, we discuss how God calls us to reach the world together as a unified body.

ON EARTH AS IT IS IN HEAVEN

As we wind down the conversation on apprenticeship to Jesus, let's zoom out. God created a vast universe. You and I are grains of sand quickly washed away by the waves of time. Life is short, and we're minuscule in the grand scheme of things. You're one of eight billion people alive today. The average person—in a lifetime—interacts with 20,000 to 80,000 people.[385] So, of the eight billion, you won't meet or interact with 99.999 percent of them. To put it another way, you will interact with 0.001 percent of humanity in your lifetime.

Knowing this, Jesus commands us to make disciples *of all nations.*[386] How? It's a physical impossibility to accomplish this *individually.* But when Jesus assigns impossible tasks, it means we need to work with him and one another to find the solution.

To follow Jesus is to *collectively* reach the lost and disciple the found. Jesus said as much:

Follow me, and I will make you fishers of men.[387]

A rough paraphrase:

As you apprentice under me together, I will form you into the kind of people who have a burden to reach the lost.

To accomplish God's will on earth starts with anguish birthed and maintained through the Holy Spirit, via consistent and fervent prayer. And anguish only comes from deep compassion. Nehemiah was devastated when he heard about the state of his people, and his compassion moved him to act. Jesus' heart was anguished when he looked over the city of Jerusalem. Anyone who has led a move of God began by seeing the need, being cut to the heart, and crying out in prayer. Pastor Jim Cymbala wrote in *Spirit Rising:*

When the Holy Spirit sets a person's life on fire, the Spirit doesn't stop there. The fire spreads, setting other people aflame too... When someone is on fire with the love of God—they love the Word and love to pray—the next thing you know, people around them are inspired to do the same... **It just happens, because it is the nature of fire to spread.**[388]

It is the nature of Jesus—and his apprentices—to spread out and reach the lost. But how? Fortunately, Jesus gave us a simple blueprint: *Invite people into the Kingdom one meal at a time.* He was onto something. Think about the last time someone invited you into their house to serve you a home-cooked meal—what did that experience communicate to you? Probably several things:

> They saw you as an equal—tables are the great equalizer.
> They treated you as a friend—tables are an offer of friendship.
> They wanted to build a relationship with you—tables invite deeper conversation.

I'm willing to bet we develop more relational depth through *one meal* than five years of passing each other by. Jesus' strategy to reach the lost is radically ordinary, beautifully simple, and fun! As we go through life and interact with others, do what Jesus would do if he were you. Invite people in. Listen attentively, ask questions, and show genuine care. See them. Jesus *asked* exponentially more questions than he *answered* and never once turned down someone searching for God.

When people see we genuinely care, they'll open up and share their story. And we can share ours. Loving isn't complicated, although it can be uncomfortable. But that's faith! We risk failure, looking foolish, or being hurt for the potential gain.

While we initially think about the challenges of doing this, there's a higher risk of *inaction*. If we live comfortable, American lives idolizing the American Dream, call Jesus Lord on Sundays only, die, and face eternity, we'll account for our inaction. We'll look God in the face and acknowledge we never loved our neighbor. Thankfully, we can begin a new journey now. Meals are no longer feasts we have in our castles, but radically ordinary opportunities for sobremesa, laden with explosive eternal potential.

The Kingdom of God is brought to earth through simple acts of love, peace, hospitality, and justice.

The best part is that we don't need permission to begin. There is no red tape. We can start now—right now—with what we have.

The way of Jesus is to love the world in small yet profound ways. This means welcoming the undeserving, serving the unworthy, and protecting the weak and vulnerable. Jesus set the standard with his life, and we can follow in his footsteps. Over time, the apprentice becomes like the teacher.[389] Even small acts of kindness and compassion inspired by Jesus can lead to incredible results. C.S. Lewis, in *Mere Christianity*, wrote:

> *Good and evil both increase at compound interest. That is why the little decisions you and I make every day are of such infinite importance. The smallest good act today is the capture of a strategic point from which, a few months later, you may be able to go on to victories you never dreamed of. An apparently trivial indulgence in lust or anger today is the loss of a ridge or railway*

line or bridgehead from which the enemy may launch an attack otherwise impossible.[390]

That's it. All it takes is one spark to start an unstoppable fire. It's the nature of fire to spread.

Are you willing to let God's Spirit work in you?

A Final Word on Perseverance

This bears repeating: as apprentices of Jesus, the goal is progress, not perfection.

We don't earn God's love—we respond to it. We're going to fall short and flat out fail at times. Like a master potter, God works slowly and methodically to craft us into people like Jesus.

Entering The Way is challenging—it's a narrow way of living, in stark contrast to the culture of the West. Reading is fun, but when you set this down, get up from the couch, and reenter society, you'll be hit. I hate to say it, but I guarantee it. There will be suffering on the road ahead. Michel de Montaigne once said:

> *We can be knowledgeable with other men's knowledge, but we cannot be wise with other men's wisdom.*[391]

In other words, there are some things you simply need to experience to learn. *When* these challenges happen, the goal is to get back up, resume your walk, and return to the practice of his Way of life.

Why did Paul and Peter write so much about problems, temptation, struggles, lust, and failure? They are realities of life. It's a marathon, not a sprint. Find your pace and begin, prayerfully dedicating each moment, minute, hour, and day to God. C.S. Lewis wrote:

> *After each failure, ask forgiveness, pick yourself up, and try again. Very often what God first helps us towards is not the virtue itself but just this power of always trying again.*[392]

If you mess up, begin again. And again. And again. Return to the steady hum of the journey.

FINAL WORD

But as the Scriptures say, 'No eye has ever seen and no ear has ever heard and it has never occurred to the human heart all the things God prepared for those who love Him.' - Paul, 1 Corinthians 2v9 (VOICE)

The world is starving for love, justice, community—for a different way of living. Like Josh the prisoner, we often shuffle through our existence shackled, silent, and resigned. But this isn't how life is supposed to be! It's short, and we're here to make an impact.

What is God's vision for the rest of your life? Close your eyes. Imagine. What will your legacy be? What will people say at your funeral? What can life—each and every day—be like if it's reoriented around Jesus? Antoine de Saint-Exupery wrote:

If you want to build a ship, don't drum up people to collect wood and don't assign them tasks and work, but rather teach them to long for the endless immensity of the sea.[393]

This is how Jesus taught—he told a story about life so compelling that we hunger and thirst for it until we find it.

If the world were full of apprentices to Jesus, societal ailments would fade away. Poverty, injustice, sex trafficking, slavery, homelessness—all would be remedied if the world were full of people of love, devoted to bringing a Kingdom to fruition here. Is this *possible*? Well, the world is only changed by people crazy enough to believe it can be.

There's new life available *here* and *now*. One of meaning and purpose that leaves a legacy and hits the mark. That life is through following Jesus—The Way—on the road less traveled. So what do you do? Convert the church? Change the world? That's God's business. Your focus must remain following his call on your life. You cannot cover the fire of God that burns through the life of a faithful apprentice. One doesn't "light a candle and put it under a basket." Instead, the fire spreads to everyone it encounters.[394]

> *As we let our own light shine, we unconsciously give other people permission to do the same.*[395]

May the way of Jesus be light to your soul.

May it cost you everything and gain you immeasurably more. May your yoke be easy and your burden light. May your steps be sure as God's sunrise dawns on your spirit, growing the burning within your heart. May God's peace, grace, and love be with you.

And may God have the last word:

> *Forget the former things; do not dwell on the past. See, I am doing a new thing! Now it springs up; do you not perceive it? I am making a way in the wilderness, and streams in the wasteland.*[396]

ENDNOTES

Bible translations and abbreviations

AMP: Amplified® Bible, Copyright © 2015 by The Lockman Foundation. Used by permission. All rights reserved. (www.Lockman.org)

ERV: Easy-to-Read Version © 2006 by Bible League International. Used by permission. All rights reserved.

ESV: English Standard Version®, copyright ©2001 by Crossway, a publishing ministry of Good News Publishers. Used by permission. All rights reserved.

MSG: The Message. Copyright ©1993, 2002, 2018 by Eugene H. Peterson. Used by permission of NavPress. All rights reserved. Represented by Tyndale House Publishers, Inc.

NIV: New International Version®, NIV®. Copyright ©1973, 1978, 1984, 2011 by Biblica, Inc.® Used by permission. All rights reserved worldwide.

NKJV: New King James Version®. Copyright ©1982 by Thomas Nelson. Used by permission. All rights reserved.

NLT: New Living Translation, copyright ©1996, 2004, 2015 by Tyndale House Foundation. Used by permission of Tyndale House Publishers, Carol Stream, Illinois 60188. All rights reserved.

NLV: New Life Version (NLV), Copyright © 1969, 2003 by Barbour Publishing, Inc.

TLB: The Living Bible. Copyright ©1971 by Tyndale House Foundation. Used by permission of Tyndale House Publishers, Carol Stream, Illinois 60188. All rights reserved.

TPT: The Passion Translation®. Copyright © 2017, 2018, 2020 by Passion & Fire Ministries, Inc. Used by permission. All rights reserved. (www.thepassiontranslation.com)

VOICE: The Voice™. Copyright © 2012 by Ecclesia Bible Society. Used by permission. All rights reserved.

1   2 Timothy 1v5–6 (NIV).

2   Willard, Dallas. *Renovation of the Heart.* NavPress, 2002, p. 15.

3   Frankl, Viktor E. *(Viktor Emil), 1905–1997. Man's Search for Meaning: An Introduction to Logotherapy. Boston: Beacon Press,* 1962.

4   Tolstoy, Leo. *What Is to Be Done?* Translated by Louise Maude and Aylmer Maude, Oxford University Press, 2010, p. 14.

5   A necessary caveat as we dive into the shared problems humanity faces. As much as I try to listen and learn from those who have had different walks, my perspective is ultimately limited to my experiences. As much as I try to listen and put myself in others' shoes, I don't truly know what it's like to grow up in El Salvador, Chuk, or Hong Kong. I know what it's like to grow up as a white middle-class male in Washington State. For the purposes of this book, while I aim to speak universally, I cannot address every experience you have had. For this, I ask your grace.

6   Thoreau, Henry David, 1817–1862. *Walden; and Civil Disobedience: Complete Texts with Introduction, Historical Contexts, Critical Essays.* Boston: Houghton Mifflin, 2000 (author's inclusion of women).

7   Sinek, Simon. *Start With Why: How Great Leaders Inspire Everyone To Take Action.* Penguin Books, 2011.

8   "Jim Carrey Quotes." *Goodreads,* www.goodreads.com/quotes/1151805-i-think-everybody-should-get-rich-and-famous-and-do. Accessed 17 Jan. 2024.

9   "Table 15. Life Expectancy at Birth, at Age 65, and at Age 75, by Sex, Race, and Hispanic Origin: United States, Selected Years 1900–2016." *CDC,* www.cdc.gov/nchs/data/hus/2017/015.pdf. Accessed 17 Jun. 2024.

10   A privilege can be something you experience because of your status or something you don't experience because of your status.

11   Brooks, David. "The Moral Bucket List." *New York Times,* 11 Apr. 2015, www.nytimes.com/2015/04/12/opinion/sunday/david-brooks-the-moral-bucket-list.html. Accessed 12 Jan. 2024.

12   Ibid.

13   Brooks, David. *The Second Mountain: The Quest for a Moral Life.* First edition. New York, Random House, 2019.

14   Willard, Dallas. *Renovation of the Heart. NavPress*, 2002, p. 19.

15   Housel, Morgan. *Same As Ever. Portfolio*, 2023, p. 240.

16   John 10v10 (NIV).

17   John 14v27 and 16v22 (NIV).

18   "Oxford English Dictionary." www.oed.com/search/dictionary/?scope=Entries&q=american+dream. Accessed 27 Dec. 2023.

19   Churchwell, Sarah. "A Brief History of the American Dream." *George W. Bush Institute*, www.bushcenter.org/catalyst/state-of-the-american-dream/churchwell-history-of-the-american-dream. Accessed 27 Dec. 2023.

20   Prodanoff, Jordan. "How Many Ads Do We See a Day? 17 Insightful Stats From 2023." *WebTribunal*, 6 Mar. 2023, webtribunal.net/blog/how-many-ads-do-we-see-a-day.

21   Ramsey, Dave. *The Total Money Makeover: A Proven Plan for Financial Fitness.* Thomas Nelson, 2003.

22   Bhutada, Govind. "The Rising Cost of College in the U.S." *Visual Capitalist*, 3 Feb. 2021, www.visualcapitalist.com/rising-cost-of-college-in-u-s.

23   "Average American Debt." *Ramsey Solutions*, 2 May 2023, www.ramseysolutions.com/debt/average-american-debt.

24   Hanson, Melanie. "Average Law School Debt." *Education Data Initiative*, 15 Jun. 2023, educationdata.org/average-law-school-debt. Accessed 28 Dec. 2023.

25   "History of U.S. Homeownership: How Housing Has Changed Since 1960." *The Zebra*, 31 Mar. 2023, www.thezebra.com/resources/home/housing-trends-visualized.

26   See above.

27   Samurai, Financial. "The Median Homebuyer Age Is Getting Older: We Better Live Longer!" *Financial Samurai*, 11 Sept. 2020, www.financialsamurai.com/the-median-homebuyer-age-is-now-so-old.

28   "Average American Debt." *Ramsey Solutions*, 2 May 2023, www. ramseysolutions.com/debt/average-american-debt.

29   Eight out of ten adults in America have at least one credit card, and 45 percent of American households carry a balance (i.e., they don't pay off their card completely each month). The average credit card debt per household with this type of debt is $14,241.

30   "Time and Busyness." *Probe*, https://probe.org/time-and-busyness. Accessed 26 Dec. 2023.

31   Comer, John Mark. *The Ruthless Elimination of Hurry* WaterBrook, 2019.

32   Conot, R. E., & Josephson, M. (2023, April 28). *Thomas Edison - American Inventor*. Encyclopædia Britannica. https://www.britannica.com/biography/Thomas-Edison/Menlo-Park.

33   Maas, Dr. James (n.d.). *Power Sleep*. The New York Times. https://archive.nytimes.com/www.nytimes.com/books/first/m/maas-sleep.html.

34   Cooper, Anderson. "What Is "Brain Hacking"? Tech Insiders on Why You Should Care." *CBS*, 9 Apr. 2017, www.cbsnews.com/news/brain-hacking-tech-insiders-60-minutes/. Accessed 27 Dec. 2023.

35   Winnick, Michael. "Putting a Finger on Our Phone Obsession." 9 Apr. 2017, https://pages.dscout.com/hubfs/downloads/dscout_mobile_touches_study_2016.pdf. Accessed 27 Dec. 2023.

36   Branka. "Average Screen Time Statistics 2023." *TrueList*, 13 Jan. 2023, truelist.co/blog/average-screen-time-statistics/.

37   Saripalli, Vara. "How to Recognize Hurry Sickness and Adopt Slow Living." *Psych Central*, 7 Apr. 2022, psychcentral.com/anxiety/always-in-a-rush-maybe-its-time-urgency#hurry-sickness. Accessed 28 Dec. 2023.

38   Lewis, C.S. *The Four Loves*. Geoffrey Bles, 1960.

39   Murthy, Vivek Dr. "Our Epidemic of Loneliness and Isolation." *Health and Human Services*, www.hhs.gov/sites/default/files/surgeon-general-social-connection-advisory.pdf. Accessed 27 Dec. 2023.

40   See Genesis 2v8 (NIV).

41   Brooks, David. *How to Know a Person. Random House*, 2023.

42   Ibid.

43   Grant, Adam. *Hidden Potential: The Science of Achieving Greater Things.* Unabridged. [New York], Penguin Audio, 2023.

44   Ibid.

45   Ibid.

46   Mayo Clinic Health System Staff. "College Students and Depression." *Mayo Clinic Health System*, 19 July 2022, www. mayoclinichealthsystem.org/hometown-health/speaking-of-health/ college-students-and-depression.

47   Mayo Foundation for Medical Education and Research." Chemical Dependency and the Physician." *Mayo Clinic Proceedings*, vol. 84, no. 7, Jul. 2009, https://www.mayoclinicproceedings.org/article/ S0025-6196(11)60751-9/fulltext.

48   Merlo, Lara J., et al. "Reasons for Misuse of Prescription Medication Among Physicians Undergoing Monitoring by a Physician Health Program." *Journal of Addiction Medicine*, vol. 7, no. 5, 2013, pp. 349-53. Abstract.

49   "Creating a Movement to Improve Well-Being in the Legal Profession." *americanbar.org*, 14 Aug. 2017, www.americanbar.org/content/dam/aba/ administrative/professional_responsibility/lawyer_well_being_report_ final.authcheckdam.pdf.

50   "Why Does Gen Z Experience Declining Religiosity?" *Reddit*, www. reddit.com/r/GenZ/comments/130tdd7/why_does_gen_z_experience_ declining_religiosity/?rdt=55009. Accessed 28 Dec. 2023.

51   Matthew 16v24–26 (NIV).

52   John 4v14 (VOICE).

53   Comer, John Mark. *Practicing the Way.* WaterBrook, 2024, p. 288.

54   Matthew 4v17 (NIV).

55   Willard, Dallas. *The Scandal of the Kingdom.* Zondervan, 2024 (includes author's paraphrase).

56   John 17v3 (NIV, author's paraphrase).

57   John 16v7–10 (NIV).

58   Ephesians 4v4–6 (NIV).

59   Ludwig Koehler et al., *The Hebrew and Aramaic Lexicon of the Old Testament* (Leiden: E.J. Brill, 1994–2000), p. 305.

60   William Arndt et al., *A Greek-English Lexicon of the New Testament and Other Early Christian Literature* (Chicago: University of Chicago Press, 2000), p. 49.

61   *Thayer's Greek Lexicon*, s.v. *"sōzō,"* Blue Letter Bible, www.blueletterbible.org/lexicon/g4982/esv/mgnt/0-1.

62   Matthew 9v22 (NIV).

63   Ignatius, "VII. Beware of False Teachers," in *The Epistle of Ignatius to the Ephesians: Shorter and Longer Versions*, in *Ante-Nicene Fathers*, vol. 1, *The Apostolic Fathers, Justin Martyr, Irenaeus*, ed. Alexander Roberts and James Donaldson, Christian Classics Ethereal.

64   Luke 5v31–32 (NIV).

65   John 4v26 (NIV) and Matthew 1v21 (NIV).

66   John 14v6 (NIV).

67   John 17v24 (NIV).

68   John 4v26 (NLT).

69   See John 1v46 (NIV).

70   See Mark 6v3 (NIV; The people retort, "Isn't this the carpenter?"). The word translated "carpenter" is *tektōn* (Greek). It means builder. There were no trees that could be used for carpentry in his area. There were plenty of rocks, however.

71   Lewis, C. S. *Mere Christianity*. William Collins, 2012.

72   1 Corinthians 15v3–8 (NIV).

73   Lincona, Michael R. *The Resurrection of Jesus: A New Historiographical Approach. Tantor Audio*, 2022.

74   Romans 10v9 (NIV).

75   Psalm 18v16–19 (NIV).

76   Acts 2v36 (NIV).

77   Gons, P. (2008, February 5). *"Savior" in Titus*. Phil Gons. Retrieved May 8, 2024, from https://philgons.com/2008/02/savior-intitus/#:~:text=It%20 occurs%20only%2024%20times,NT%20occurrences%20are%20 in%20Titus.&text=Second%2C%20it%20occurs%20three%20 times,the%20Son%20as%20our%20Savior.

78   Matthew 16v24 (NIV).

79   Matthew 11v28–30 (NIV; author's note added in brackets).

80   Comer, *Practicing the Way*. WaterBrook, 2024, p. 288.

81   See "Lexicon:: Strong's G3101 - MathēTēs." *Blue Letter Bible*, www. blueletterbible.org/lexicon/g3101/niv/mgnt/0-1/. See also: "Lexicon:: Strong's G5546 - Christianos." *Blue Letter Bible*, www.blueletterbible. org/lexicon/g5546/kjv/tr/0-1/.

82   See Matthew 28v18–20 (NIV).

83   See Luke 6v40 (NIV).

84   Matthew 16v24 (NIV).

85   Foster, Richard J. *Celebration of Discipline: The Path to Spiritual Growth*. 3rd ed. [San Francisco, CA], HarperSanFrancisco, 1998.

86   Galatians 5v24 (NIV).

87   "A History of Woody Allen and Soon-Yi Previn Describing Their Relationship, from "the Heart Wants What It Wants" to "I Was Paternal"." *Salon*, 30 Jul. 2015, www.salon.com/2015/07/30/a_history_ of_woody_allen_and_soon_yi_previn_describing_their_relationship_ from_the_heart_wants_what_it_wants_to_i_was_paternal/. Accessed 22 Jan. 2024.

88   See Romans 7v15–20 (NIV).

89   Covey, Stephen M.R. *The Speed of Trust: The One Thing That Changes Everything / Stephen M. R. Covey*. Free Press: New York, 2006. Text.

90   Ephesians 5v18 (NIV).

91   Matthew 11v29 (NIV).

92   Philippians 2v12 (NIV).

93   See Ephesians 5v18 and Galatians 5v25 (NIV).

94   Groeschel, Craig. *Think Ahead. Zondervan*, 2024, p. 288.

95   John 15 (NIV).

96   Unfortunately, I've tested this theory and hit the wall at mile 18—not fun!

97   Willard, Dallas. *The Great Omission: Reclaiming Jesus's Essential Teachings On Discipleship*. [San Francisco, Calif.], HarperSanFrancisco, 2006, p. 86.

98   1 Corinthians 9v25–27 (NIV).

99   Medina, Mark. "'He's in Love with Getting Better': How Stephen Curry Has Maintained Peak Conditioning." *NBA.Com*, 13 Jun. 2022, www.nba. com/news/how-stephen-curry-maintains-peak-conditioning. Accessed 4 Mar. 2024.

100 Wallace, Doug. "Steph Curry Brain Training." *Gaia Health Blog*, www. gaiahealthblog.com/2017/03/03/steph-curry-brain-training/. Accessed 20 Dec. 2023.

101 Dubs By the Numbers: Stephen Curry First to 4,000 Career 3-Pointers." NBA.com, 13 Mar. 2025, https://www.nba.com/warriors/news/dubs-by-the-numbers-stephen-curry-first-to-4000-career-3-pointers-20250313.

102 Practicing the Way provides a free tool called the Rule of Life Builder. Visit practicingtheway.org.

103 Foster, *Celebration of Discipline*, p. 3.

104 Staton, Tyler. *Praying Like Monks, Living Like Fools: An Invitation to the Wonder and Mystery of Prayer. Zondervan*, 2022, p. 272.

105 Isaiah 26v3 (MSG).

106 Psalm 1v2 (NIV).

107 1 Thessalonians 5v17 (NIV).

108 John 15v1–15 (NIV).

109 Brother Lawrence, and John J. Delaney. *The Practicing of the Presence of God. Image Books/Doubleday*, 1977, p. 100.

110 Ibid.

111 Mark 1v35 (NIV).

112 Luke 6v12 (NIV).

113 John 11v38–44 (NIV).

114 There were 5,000 men, so counting women and children, the number was likely around 15,000 people.

115 Matthew 14v23 (NIV).

116 Mark 6v31–46 (NIV).

117 Matthew 26v38–39 (NIV).

118 Luke 22v44 (NIV). This is a scientifically recorded phenomenon which occurs when a person is under *extreme* stress and anxiety.

119 Mark 1v9–10 (NIV)

120 John 1v32 (NIV).

121 John 11v42 (NIV)

122 John 16v7 (AMP).

123 Deuteronomy 31v6 (NIV).

124 Willard, Dallas. *Hearing God. IVP*, 2012, p. 145.

125 See Numbers 12v6–8 (NIV).

126 John 10v27 (NIV).

127 1 John 1v6 (NIV).

128 1 Samuel 16v14 (NIV).

129 Nouwen, Henri. *Here and Now. PublishDrive*, 2006.

130 Lewis, C.S. "Reflections: Half-Hearted Creatures." *C.S. Lewis Institute*, 1 Oct. 2008, www.cslewisinstitute.org/resources/reflections-november 2008/#:~:text=We%20are%20half%2Dhearted%20creatures,are%20far%20 too%20easily%20pleased.

131 Newport, Cal. *Deep Work: Rules for Focused Success in a Distracted World*. First edition. New York, Grand Central Publishing, 2016.

132 Luke 10v38–42 (NIV).

133 Piper, John. "If I Could Start All Over: Six Lessons for Your Twenties." *Desiring God*, 11 Apr. 2018, www.desiringgod.org/messages/if-i-could-start-all-over. Accessed 26 Dec. 2023.

134   1 Peter 3v12 (NIV).

135   Lewis, C. S. *Mere Christianity*. William Collins, 2012.

136   Luke 22v39 (NIV).

137   Munoz, N. (2023, March 19). *The Power of Stillness: Finding Serenity Amidst Acceleration*. Medium. Retrieved January 30, 2024, from https://medium.com/conscious-connection/the-power-of-stillness-finding-serenity-amidst-acceleration-848907bc56ce.

138   Villodas, Rich. *The Deeply Formed Life*. WaterBrook, 2020.

139   1 Kings 19v13 (NIV).

140   Isaiah 30v15 (NIV).

141   Psalm 98v4 (NIV).

142   Romans 8v26 (NIV).

143   Nouwen, Henri J. M.. *The Way of the Heart: Desert Spirituality and Contemporary Ministry*. Cambridge: HarperSanFrancisco, 1981.

144   Nouwen, Henri J. *Reaching Out: The Three Movements of the Spiritual Life*. Image Books, 1986, p. 165.

145   Luke 5v15–16 (NIV).

146   Matthew 6v6 (NIV).

147   Psalm 23v2–3 (NIV).

148   Psalm 37v7 (NIV).

149   Psalm 46v1 (NIV).

150   1 Samuel 3v4 (NIV).

151   We're living in a similar "exile" now—existing within a foreign culture looking to shape and mold us into people with a distinct set of values.

152   Daniel 6v10 (MSG).

153   Psalm 55v16–17 (ERV).

154   See Acts 2v15 (Peter prayed at the third hour of the day, or 9:00 AM), Acts 10v9 (Peter prayed at the sixth hour of the day, or noon), and Acts 3v1 (Peter and John prayed at the ninth hour, or 3:00 PM, NIV)

155   Acts 10 (NIV).

156 St. Benedict, for instance, ordered parts of the book of Psalms to be recited at seven points of the day, every day. He said: "To pray is to work, to work is to pray." The modern word "office" comes from the Latin word "opus," meaning work. To Benedict, set prayer was our daily work.

157 Peter Scazzero, *Emotionally Healthy Spirituality: It's Impossible to Be Spiritually Mature, While Remaining Emotionally Immature* Zondervan, 2017.

158 See Acts 4v23–30 (NIV).

159 Postell, Marissa. "The State of Quiet Time: Who's Most Likely to Practice Daily Devotions." *Christianity Today*, 3 Jan. 2023, www.christianitytoday.com/news/2023/january/daily-quiet-time-god-prayer-bible-reading-lifeway-survey.html. Accessed 4 Jun. 2024.

160 Matthew 6v9–13 (NIV). We find a shorter version of Jesus' model prayer in Luke as well, but for purposes of this section, we use Matthew's version because it is more expansive.

161 Matthew 6v33 (NIV).

162 2 Corinthians 4v16–18 (NIV).

163 "Saint Augustine Quotes." *AZ Quotes*, www.azquotes.com/quote/662102.

164 Philippians 2v21 (NIV).

165 1 John 5v14–15 (NLT).

166 Ephesians 4v32 (NIV).

167 Psalm 32v4–6 (NIV).

168 1 Peter 3v9 (NIV).

169 James 1v14–15 (NIV).

170 1 Corinthians 10v13 (NIV).

171 1 Corinthians 6v18 (NIV).

172 Jeremiah 15v16 (NIV).

173 Hebrews 4v12 (NIV).

174 Isaiah 55v10–11 (NIV).

175 Jeremiah 20v9 (NIV).

176   See Psalm 42 and Matthew 5 (NIV).

177   Jeremiah 1v17 (NIV).

178   Habakkuk 2v2 (NIV).

179   Revelation 1v19 (NIV).

180   Luke 24v26–27 (MSG).

181   Luke 24v32 (NIV).

182   Foster, *Celebration of Discipline*, p. 63. His recommended list of Classics in the section on "Study" is powerful.

183   John 1v14 (NIV).

184   Deuteronomy 17v18–20 (NIV).

185   1 Peter 2v9–12 (NIV).

186   1 Corinthians 3v16 (NIV).

187   Exodus 13v21–22 (NIV).

188   Matthew 7v13–14 (NIV).

189   Nieuwhof, Carey. *At Your Best*. WaterBrook, 2021.

190   Zechariah 7v5 (NIV).

191   Tarrants, Thomas A. "The Placing of Fasting in the Christian Life." *C.S. Lewis Institute*, 6 Jun. 2018, www.cslewisinstitute.org/resources/the-place-of-fasting-in-the-christian-life/. Accessed 26 Feb. 2024.

192   See 2 Chronicles 20v1–4 (NIV) and Ezra 8v21–23 (NIV).

193   "Didache." *The Catholic Encyclopedia*.Vol. 4. New York: Robert Appleton Company, 1908.

194   Matthew 9v14 (NIV).

195   Matthew 9v14–15 (NIV).

196   Matthew 9v16 (NIV).

197   Acts 13v2 (NIV).

198   2 Corinthians 6v4–10 and 11v23–28 (NIV).

199   Matthew 6v16–18 (MSG).

200   Luke 4v2 (NIV).

201   Matthew 4v1–2 (NIV).

202   John 14v26 (NIV).

203   Acts 1v8 (NIV).

204   John 16v8 (NIV).

205   Mulholland, Robert, and Kaleo Griffith. *Invitation to a Journey: A Road Map for Spiritual Formation* Unabridged, Intervarsity Press, 2023.

206   Matthew 6v5 (MSG).

207   Proverbs 21v2 (NIV).

208   Psalm 139v2–3 (NIV).

209   James 5v16 (TPT).

210   Psalm 51v16–17 (NIV).

211   Matthew 6v3–4 (NIV).

212   Matthew 5v8 (NIV).

213   Psalm 139v23–24 (NIV).

214   Credit to John Mark Comer for this phrase, although I cannot find the location of where he said it.

215   Comer, John Mark. *Four Layers of Sin.* 2024.

216   Matthew 13v44 (NIV).

217   Willard, Dallas. *Renovation of the Heart. NavPress,* 2002, p. 68.

218   Romans 12v2 (NIV).

219   Galatians 4v19 (NIV).

220   Willard, Dallas. *Renovation of the Heart. NavPress,* 2002, p. 14.

221   "3339. Metamorphoó." *Bible Hub,* biblehub.com/greek/3339.htm. Accessed 20 Dec. 2023.

222   Grant, Adam. *Hidden Potential: The Science of Achieving Greater Things.* Unabridged. [New York], Penguin Audio, 2023.

223   Clear, James. "The Habits Guide: How to Build Good Habits and Break Bad Ones." *James Clear,* https://jamesclear.com/habits. Accessed 20 Dec. 2023.

224   Galatians 5v1 (NIV, author's paraphrase)

225   Matthew 12v43–45 (NIV).

226   "Spiritual Formation in Christ for the Whole Life and Whole Person" in *Vocatio,* Vol. 12, no. 2, Spring, 2001, p. 7

227   Luke 2v52 (NIV).

228   Psalm 139v23 (NIV).

229   Philippians 4v6 (NIV).

230   Philippians 4v6 (author's paraphrase)

231   2 Corinthians 10v5 (NIV).

232   Philippians 4v6–7 (TPT).

233   Hebrews 4v15 (NIV).

234   Proverbs 23v7 (NKJV).

235   Isaacson, Walter. *Steve Jobs. Simon & Schuster*, 2011, p. 630.

236   Galatians 3v26 (NIV).

237   Psalm 139v14 (VOICE).

238   As noted above in footnote 68, see Mark 6v3 (The people retort, "Isn't this the carpenter?"). The word translated 'carpenter' is *tektōn* (Greek) which means builder. There were no trees that could be used for carpentry in his area, but there were plenty of rocks.

239   Luke 3v21–22 (NIV).

240   Zephaniah 3v17 (author's paraphrase).

241   Matthew 18v1–4 (NIV).

242   Mark 10v3–16 (MSG).

243   Acts 17v1 (NLT)

244   Brown, Brene. *Dare to Lead*. Vermilion, 2018.

245   Psalm 131v1–3 (TPT).

246   Matthew 20v29–34 (NIV).

247   Luke 1v78–79 (MSG).

248   Galatians 5v22–23 (ESV)

249   Galatians 5v19–21 (TPT).

250   John 14v15 (NIV).

251   Willard, Dallas. *Renovation of the Heart*. NavPress, 2002, p. 25.

252   "Humans Are…Trees?" *BibleProject*, 6 Jan. 2020, bibleproject.com/podcast/humans-are-trees/. Accessed 10 Jan. 2023.

253   Psalm 92v12–15 (NIV).

254 Matthew 7v17–18 (NIV).

255 1 Corinthians 1v10–17 and 11v1 (NIV).

256 Ephesians 4v15 (ESV).

257 John 21v18–19 (NIV, author's paraphrase)

258 St. Basil the Great. *On Christian Doctrine and Practice. St Vladimir's Seminary Pr*, 2013, p. 324.

259 Ibid.

260 Ibid.

261 Numbers 12v3 (NIV).

262 Ibid.

263 Philippians 3v15 (NIV).

264 Quoted in: Rolheiser, Ronald. *Sacred Fire. Image*, 2017.

265 Zechariah 4v10 (NLT)

266 Howard Rachinski's book *Perpetual* is a helpful guide to understanding seven types of seasons everyone will experience in life.

267 Ecclesiastes 3v1 (AMP).

268 Psalm 31v15 (NLV).

269 Exodus 33v1–3 (NIV).

270 Exodus 33v15–17 (NIV).

271 Matthew 11:28–30 (MSG)

272 Exodus 20v10 (NIV).

273 See James 2v24 and Romans 3v28 (NIV).

274 James 2v19 (NIV).

275 Willard, Dallas. *The Great Omission: Reclaiming Jesus's Essential Teachings On Discipleship.* (San Francisco, Calif.), HarperSanFrancisco, 2006.

276 Matthew 4v19 (NIV).

277 Mathew 16v18 (NIV).

278 2 Corinthians 6v1 (NLT).

279 Matthew 5v13 (NIV).

280 Acts 8v26 (NLT).

281 Acts 8v27 (NLT).

282 Acts 8v29 (NLT).

283 Isaiah 53v7–8 and Acts 8v32–33 (NLT).

284 A helpful commentary on this concept can be found in Dallas Willard's *Hearing God. IVP*, 2012, p. 268–271.

285 Matthew 25v14–30 (NIV).

286 Matthew 25v21, 23 (ESV).

287 Matthew 25v24–30 (ESV).

288 John 15 (NIV).

289 Matthew 13v23 (ESV)

290 Schopenhauer, Arthur. *The World As Will and Representation. Dover Pub.*

291 Romans 8v28 (NIV).

292 Covey, Stephen R. *The 7 Habits of Highly Effective People: Restoring the Character Ethic.* [Rev. ed.]. Free Press, 2004.

293 Luke 21v3–4 (NKJV).

294 Philippians 4v9 (NIV).

295 2 Corinthians 1v21 (NIV).

296 Philippians 1v6 (NIV).

297 Daniel 10v12 (NIV). It turns out there was a spiritual battle happening over the region Daniel was praying for, preventing a sooner response.

298 Schapelhouman, Henriet. "Billy Graham: Fruit Grows In Valleys." *Henriet's Blog*, 13 Aug. 2010, *Billy Graham: Fruit Grows In Valleys.* Accessed 21 May 2024.

299 Joshua 21 (NIV).

300 Matthew 22v36–40 (NIV).

301 Matthew 7v21–23 (NIV).

302 Matthew 25v29 (NIV).

303 Ecclesiastes 11v4 (AMP).

304 James 1v5 (AMP).

305 Luke 10v29 (NIV, paraphrased).

306 See John 1 (the Word became (*ginomai*) flesh. Or Luke 6: a disciple isn't above his teacher, but everyone when he is fully trained will become (*ginomai*) like his teacher.

307 "Road to Jericho (Setting for the Good Samaritan)." *FaithND*, faith. nd.edu/s/1210/faith/interior.aspx?sid=1210&gid=609&pgid=33100. Accessed 5 Jan. 2023.

308 Luke 10v30–35 (NIV).

309 1 John 3v16–17 (MSG).

310 Luke 5v31–32 (NIV).

311 John 13v34–35 (TLB)

312 Acts 3v1–8 (NIV).

313 2 Thessalonians 3v10 (NIV).

314 *Dictionary.com*, www.dictionary.com/browse/discernment. Accessed 5 Jan. 2023.

315 "What Is Spiritual Discernment? Its Signs and Power Explained." *Pray.com*, www.pray.com/articles/what-is-spiritual-discernment-its-signs-and-power-explained. Accessed 5 Jan. 2023.

316 See Matthew 10v16 for instance.

317 Matthew 7v1–2 (NIV).

318 Boom, Corrie. "Guideposts Classics: Corrie Ten Boom on Forgiveness." *Guideposts*, guideposts.org/positive-living/guideposts-classics-corrie-ten-boom-forgiveness/. Accessed 4 Apr. 2024.

319 Matthew 5v43–45 (NIV).

320 Matthew 5v43–45 (NIV).

321 Thomas Merton, *No Man Is an Island* (1955)

322 Hebrews 4v15–16 (MSG).

323 Elkin, Eric. "Am I A Sheep?" *Ordinary Voices*, ordinaryvoices.org/reflect/am-i-a-sheep. Accessed 6 Jan. 2023.

324 Matthew 25v35–40 (NIV).

325   Acts 9v4 (NIV).

326   Dunbar, Robin. *Friends: Understanding the Power of Our Most Important Relationships.* Little, Brown UK, 2022, p. 432.

327   Thompson, Helen. *This Book Could Fix Your Life.* John Murray, 2022.

328   "Dunbar's Number: Why We Can Only Maintain 150 Relationships." *BBC,* 9 Oct. 2019, www.bbc.com/future/article/20191001-dunbars-number-why-we-can-only-maintain-150-relationships. Accessed 9 Apr. 2024.

329   Starendal, Carl. "The Dunbar Number." *Medium,* 12 May 2014, cstarendal.medium.com/the-dunbar-number-40c826da34c3. Accessed 9 Apr. 2024.

330   See Titus 1v4 and 1 Timothy 1v2.

331   John 10v10 (NIV).

332   1 Corinthians 15v6 (NIV).

333   Acts 1v15 (NIV).

334   Luke 10v1 (NIV).

335   See Matthew 16v13–20 (NIV).

336   Mark 5v37–43 (NIV).

337   Mark 9v9 and Matthew 17 (NIV).

338   Dawes, Zach Jr. "Global Christian Population Projected to Reach 3.3 Billion by 2050." *Good Faith Media,* 13 Feb. 2023, goodfaithmedia.org/global-christian-population-projected-to-reach-3-3-billion-by-2050/. Accessed 27 Nov. 2023.

339   John Mark Comer's *Practicing The Way* website (practicingtheway.org) is a free resource in this regard.

340   Nieuwhof, Carey. "5 Powerful Ways Becoming A Morning Person Unlocks Your Leadership." *Carey Nieuwhof,* careynieuwhof.com/5-powerful-ways-becoming-a-morning-person-unlocks-your-leadership/. Accessed 8 Apr. 2024.

341   "Reflections: First and Second Things." *C.S. Lewis Institute,* 1 Jul. 2017, www.cslewisinstitute.org/resources/reflections-july-2017/. Accessed 6 Jan. 2023.

342 Krockow, Eva M. Ph.D. "How Many Decisions Do We Make Each Day?" *Psychology Today*, 27 Sept. 2018, www.psychologytoday.com/us/blog/stretching-theory/201809/how-many-decisions-do-we-make-each-day. Accessed 6 Jan. 2023.

343 TerKeurst, Lysa. *Good Boundaries and Goodbyes*. Thomas Nelson, 2022, p. 256.

344 Brooks, David. *How to Know a Person*. Random House, 2023.

345 Matthew 17v1–5 (NIV).

346 Ibid.

347 Matthew 23v37 (MSG).

348 Revelation 3v20 (AMP).

349 Luke 10v5–6 (NIV).

350 Nouwen, Henri. *The Genesee Diary: Report from a Trappist Monastery*. Image, 1981, p. 224.

351 Gandhi, Mahatma. "Mahatma Gandhi Quotes." *Goodreads*, www.goodreads.com/quotes/22155-i-like-your-christ-i-do-not-like-your-christians. Accessed 6 May 2024.

352 Sam Rayburn, Quoted by Mark Shields, PBS Evening News, October 13, 2017. *Eigen's Political and Historical Quotations* (note: paraphrased)

353 See Matthew 4v19 (NIV).

354 Green, Joel B., and Scot McKnight, eds. *Dictionary of Jesus and the Gospels*. Downers Grove: InterVarsity Press, 1992, p. 781.

355 Bacher, Wilhelm, and Lewis N. Dembitz. "Synagogue." *Jewish Encyclopedia*, www.jewishencyclopedia.com/articles/14160-synagogue. Accessed 6 Jan. 2023.

356 The full prayer consists of Deuteronomy 6v4, 11v13–21, and Numbers 15v37–41)

357 Green and McKnight, *Dictionary of Jesus and the Gospels*, p. 783.

358 Luke 4v16–17 (NIV).

359 See Matthew 4v23 (NIV), Luke 4v33–35 and Mark 3v1–5 (NIV).

360 John 8v29 (NIV).

361 Matthew 13v54 and Luke 4v16–30 (NIV).

362 Exodus 20v8–11 (NIV).

363 "Attendance at Religious Services." *Pew Research Center*, www.pewresearch.org/religious-landscape-study/database/attendance-at-religious-services/. Accessed 21 May 2024.

364 John 9v22 (NIV).

365 John 19v14–16 (NIV)

366 Acts 5v17–18 and 6v59–60 (NIV).

367 Matthew 28v19–20 and Luke 24v45–49 (NIV).

368 Matthew 26v26–29 and 1 Corinthians 11v23–26 (NIV).

369 Acts 2

370 Acts 20v7 (NIV).

371 John 20v1, John 20v15–18, Matthew 28v1, Matthew 28v9–10 (NIV).

372 Acts 11v26 (NIV).

373 1 Corinthians 15v9 (NIV).

374 Acts 2v42–47 (NIV).

375 1 Corinthians 2v1–5 (MSG).

376 Foster, *Celebration of Discipline*, p. 144.

377 Bonhoeffer, Dietrich, and Clyde E. Fant. *Bonhoeffer: Worldly Preaching*. *T. Nelson*, 1975, p. 92.

378 Fant 1975, 138, 149.

379 Breen, Mike. "Obituary for the American Church." *Mission Frontiers*, 1 July. 2012, www.missionfrontiers.org/issue/article/obituary-for-the-american-church.

380 Revelation 3v14–20 (NIV).

381 Matthew 16v18 (NIV).

382 Acts 20v28 (NIV).

383 Isaiah 56v7 (NIV).

384 Ephesians 5v27 (NIV).

385 Note: The average life expectancy is 78.3 years, and we remember

people we meet after age five. Assuming we interact with three new people daily in cities, we get the following formula: (78.3 - 5) x 3 x 365.24 = 80,000 people.

386   Matthew 28v19–20 (NIV)

387   Matthew 4v19 (NIV).

388   Cymbala, Jim. *Spirit Rising. Zondervan*, 2012, p. 71.

389   Luke 6v40 (AMP).

390   Lewis, C. S. *Mere Christianity*. William Collins, 2012.

391   "Thoughts on the Business of Life." *ForbesQuotes*, www.forbes.com/ quotes/6818/.

392   Lewis, C. S. *Mere Christianity*. William Collins, 2012.

393   de Saint-Exupery, Antoine. *The Little Prince*. Translated by Irene Testot-Ferry, Wordsworth Editions, 2018.

394   Matthew 5v15 (author's paraphrase).

395   Williamson, Marianne. *A Return to Love: Reflections on the Principles of a Course in Miracles*. Harper Collins, 1992. pp. Chapter 7, Section 3.

396   Isaiah 43v18–19 (NIV).

ABOUT THE AUTHOR

Gabe Foster, born and raised in Vancouver, Washington, is a pastor, writer, and attorney with a multifaceted background and a deep passion for spiritual formation. *The Fire Within* is his first book, and he is committed to helping followers of Jesus build intentional, resilient lives that reflect the beauty and strength of Christ. Gabe earned his law degree from the University of Washington School of Law and subsequently served as a prosecuting attorney, gaining valuable insight into the complexities of human experience. Now, he serves as a pastor at Mannahouse Church in Vancouver, Washington, where he finds fulfillment in guiding and supporting the congregation. Drawing from Scripture, personal stories, legal training, and lived experience, Gabe writes with clarity, warmth, and a profound love for the Church. He resides in the Pacific Northwest with his wife, Roseanne, and their four children, Andrew, Evelyn, Daniel, and Michael.